The
MOTHER OF GOD
and
HER GLORIOUS FEASTS

THE MOTHER OF GOD

The
MOTHER OF GOD
and
HER GLORIOUS FEASTS

by

Father H. O'Laverty, B.A.

"My soul doth magnify the Lord. And my spirit hath rejoiced in God my Saviour. Because he hath regarded the humility of his handmaid; for behold from henceforth all generations shall call me blessed. Because he that is mighty, hath done great things to me; and holy is his name. And his mercy is from generation unto generations, to them that fear him."

—Luke 1:46-50

TAN BOOKS AND PUBLISHERS, INC.
Rockford, Illinois 61105

Nihil Obstat: Alb. Boone, S.J.
                  Bruges, Belgium
                  May 28, 1925

Imprimatur: ✝ J. Van der Meersch
                  Bruges, Belgium
                  June 27, 1925

This book was originally published between 1908 and approximately 1915 under the title, *The Mother of God's Glorious Feasts*. It was reprinted in 1925 and later reprinted again in 1977 by Marian Publications, South Bend, Indiana. The present edition, done in 1987 under the new title, has been retypeset by TAN Books and Publishers, Inc.

Library of Congress Catalog Card No.: 87-50580

ISBN: 0-89555-317-1

The cover picture is the Icon of Vladimir, painted in 1120 in Constantinople and taken to Russia in 1130.

Cover design by Peter Massari.

Printed and bound in the United States of America.

TAN BOOKS AND PUBLISHERS, INC.
P.O. Box 424
Rockford, Illinois 61105

1987

DEDICATION

This book has been reprinted by the Publishers in honor of the Blessed Virgin Mary and is dedicated as a gift to her for the Special Marian Year—June 7, 1987 through August 15, 1988. May it inspire in her children a greater knowledge and understanding of her role in our redemption and in our salvation, and may it instill in us a greater love for her in our lives.

OUR LADY, QUEEN OF THE MISSIONS

CONTENTS

THE MOTHER OF OUR SAVIOUR

PUBLISHER'S PREFACE

The Unusual Merits of This Book

THE MOTHER OF GOD AND HER GLORIOUS FEASTS is truly one of the rarest books about Mary, or about the Faith, that the Catholic reader is likely ever to encounter. For this little treatise is about one of the most sublime mysteries of our Faith—the role of the Mother of God in our redemption and in our salvation—but also, and perhaps just as importantly, it is about our Faith in general. Basing his approach upon the major feasts and titles of Our Blessed Mother, the author has examined in these pages the life and mission of Mary, but in the process, he has also given a beautiful and wise commentary on the Catholic life and how we should live it.

Here the reader will discover the reasons for Mary's greatness and pre-eminence stated perhaps better and more simply than in any other book about Our Lord's Holy Mother: She was born free from Original Sin, and further, during her entire life she never committed even the slightest sin. Also, she received more graces than anyone else who ever lived, and she accepted and corresponded to them all. Consequently, her growth in holiness was in a manner that one might best describe as "geometric." Further, as the author points out, Our Blessed Lord did not give Mary special instructions and special considerations during her life, but made her wait and wonder what was to be, just as we must do—and this in order to allow her to gain all possible graces by her humility, submission, patience and confidence.

Fr. O'Laverty debunks many notions we often generally assume about Mary that he says are just not true; for example, that she had continual mystical experiences. The author claims she had but one, that being the

Annunciation of the Angel Gabriel that she was to be the Mother of the Saviour. Further, the author denies that Our Lord worked special miracles for her and that He confided to her many things that were to occur in His life. Instead, as the author maintains, Our Lord let Mary remain in question as to what would transpire, that she might gain the more in grace and in spiritual advancement by her patient, resigned "living-through" all the mysteries of His work of Redemption.

It will take only a chapter or two for the reader to understand how privileged he is to be reading the sublime thoughts of a truly profound and wise writer, and that he is reading not just about Our Blessed Mother and her role in our redemption and in our salvation, but also about many of the principal tenets of our Faith and about profound truths of life scored in both the Old and New Testaments—but generally ignored and violated today.

Too, *The Mother of God and Her Glorious Feasts* is one of those truly unusual books that satisfies both the intellect and the heart, that appeals to the mind and to the emotions. It is a book that will evoke tears of love and appreciation and that will make the reader aware that Mary was and is a real person, one with whom each of us can truly identify. The reader will come away with a profound appreciation of the suffering endured by the Blessed Virgin Mary and why therefore she enjoys such an exalted place in Heaven—and why therefore she is so pre-eminently powerful before the throne of God in obtaining help for her children when they call upon her in their need.

The reader will have reaped a rich reward if he will have derived no other benefit from this book than the realization it is from sufferings that come blessings, and from the greatest sufferings—as in the life of Jesus and Mary—that come the greatest spiritual rewards. Most people try to dodge sufferings; whereas, they are part and parcel of this vale of tears. Most people rail at sufferings; whereas, they are the stuff of our spiritual growth. Complaining will not make suffering disappear but only make it more difficult to bear. The proper attitude toward suffering is to treat it as Mary did—with acceptance, humility, resignation and conformity to God's holy will, offering to her Divine Son all our merits derived from such sufferings properly accepted and interiorized.

Such a holy appreciation about Mary and about our Faith can be derived from this book that it is difficult to render it justice. Alone the insight about the difference between natural and supernatural acts will make the book worth reading. Few people today realize that, however good and noteworthy such may be, actions performed while not in the state of grace are of absolutely no value for eternity. We must be in God's grace to gain merit for the next life from the good which we do here on earth. Too often we may think that "John" or "Mary" are "good" people and that they are solidly on the path to Heaven because of their "good works"; whereas, just the opposite may be true because they are not in the state of grace and therefore that they actually stand in great need of our prayers.

Then too, Father O'Laverty points out that we today who attend the Holy Sacrifice of the Mass devoutly and receive Holy Communion actually are more blessed and more privileged than those who stood with Jesus at the foot of the Cross on Calvary, for we too, as did they, witness the Redemption of the world (re-enacted or represented on our altars by the special power of the priest at Mass), but we, unlike those beneath the Cross on Golgotha, can actually receive the Body, Blood, Soul and Divinity of our Saviour and be transformed thereby into the likeness of Him which He desires to create in us.

This book is indeed a great grace, especially reappearing in print as it is during a period of confusion, ignorance and falling-away from the Catholic Faith. It must have been a special prompting of the Holy Ghost that inspired Pope John Paul II to declare the Special Marian Year from Pentecost Sunday, June 7, 1987 through the Feast of the Assumption, August 15, 1988. Hopefully, this book can continue in print for many years beyond this present Marian Year, but appearing as it is just prior to that signal event, may it receive as a result of the Marian Year the widest possible distribution, and may the dedicated children of Mary distribute copies far and wide, that the glories of this glorious Mother of us all might become universally recognized throughout the Church and throughout the world and that people everywhere will once more call upon the Mother of God in all their needs and in all their tribulations, that she might reign universally as "Queen of Heaven and Earth" and that she might be recognized by all as "our life, our sweetness and our hope."

Thomas A. Nelson
Publisher
May 13, 1987
On the 70th Anniversary of
Our Lady's first apparition at Fatima

AUTHOR'S PREFACE

The Purpose of this Book

FOR thirty years out of the thirty-three years of His mortal life, Jesus lived with the holiest creature that ever this world saw or heard of. During these years, the deep and supernatural love of Jesus for His sweet Mother was developed and perfected, and He gave her a willing and perfect obedience. Surely she, who had the privilege to command God Himself, is worthy of special honor and devotion. Her example must be worth following when the Son of God lived with her during the greater part of His life. And as she then had only to express a wish in order to have it carried out by her Divine Son, so now her power in Heaven is not lessened, but rather increased. Devotion to Mary has always been regarded by the saints as a sure sign of predestination. The chief object of the cultivation of the love and veneration of Our Lady is to develop within our souls the interior life of grace. Mary is the model of the interior life, and this is after all the important life. Worldly success is passing, but the acquisition of grace is lasting and is really the only thing in this world that is worth troubling about. Devotion to Mary means the development of this interior life of grace. In vain will we search for a single soul which is truly interior or which has reached great sanctity which has not had a deep love for Mary and which has not had experience of her sweet protection and assistance. In vain will we search for one who has been devout to Mary and yet has not reached great heights of sanctity before death. Mary will never allow one of her children to perish, nor will she fail them in their hour of need.

The great and glorious feasts of Mary are too often forgotten or neglected. Her dolors are not sufficiently meditated upon, nor are they appreciated by the majority of the faithful. It is much better not to separate Jesus from Mary. During life they were together, and they are together in Heaven. In the Holy Eucharist the Body and Blood of Jesus which we receive is the same which Jesus took from Mary. Without Mary we would have had no Redemption.

The following pages are the outcome of the author's personal love for the Mother of Jesus, and he offers them as an act of homage to Our Lady in recognition of all the graces he has received through her intercession.

The
MOTHER OF GOD
and
HER GLORIOUS FEASTS

OUR LADY OF MERCY

A PRAYER-POEM

Child of Mary

Child of Mary, name of honor,
  Prouder far than kingly crown;
God Himself, to win that title
  From His heavenly throne came down.

He, the first-born Child of Mary,
  Calls us to His Mother's side,
Shares with us His dearest treasure,
  "Mother, 't was for these I died."

O Immaculate, Unfallen,
  Tarnished by no breath of sin,
Yet, I dare to call thee "Mother";
  Open, Mother, let me in.

Thou, of mercy's self art Mother,
  And thy heart is meek and mild;
Open wide thy arms and take me
  As a mother takes her child.

Child of Mary, may my feelings,
  Thoughts, words, deeds, and heart's desires,
All befit a lowly creature
  Who to such high name aspires.

Ne'er shall sin (for sin could only)
  From my sinless Mother sever;
Mary's Child till death shall call me,
  Child of Mary then forever.

THE IMMACULATE CONCEPTION

CHAPTER 1

The Immaculate Conception

M ANY years elapsed from the Fall of our first parents until the Redeemer promised to Adam appeared visibly in the world, and it may seem strange that God delayed so long in fulfilling His promise to send the Messias who was to restore all that was lost by the Fall. We see in this delay the manifestation of divine wisdom, which always prepares the world and the individual soul for the graces and blessings to be given to mankind. The Redeemer was to give back to the human race all that it had lost by the sin of our first parents. In reality, the Redemption has not only restored to us all we lost, but it has been so copious that we have gained far more than ever we lost, and indeed the Fall of Adam and Eve has been a great blessing for us. It is a blessing because Christ has suffered so much that it is now quite easy to reach a great degree of glory for eternity, and the very evils or temporal afflictions caused by the Fall of our first parents can now be used to increase our merit and so increase our glory for Heaven.

Millions are now enjoying the Beatific Vision of God and are filled with unspeakable happiness simply because they bore patiently, by the aid of grace, the few little sufferings of this life for a few short years. In this way we have reason to rejoice because of the goodness of Jesus, who gained so many graces for us by His sufferings and death. The delay in the coming of the Messias did not mean that those who lived before His arrival had no means of salvation. They certainly had far fewer graces than we now have, because we are members of the True Church and we have Our Lord in the Blessed Eucharist for our spiritual food or for the preservation and for the increase of grace in our souls, but still those who lived before Christ received graces in view of the merits of the Passion and Death of Our Lord.

We must go deeper than all this to find the real cause of the thousands of years of delay in the fulfillment of the promise made to Adam and Eve. In reality, it took all those years to prepare for the visible presence of the Saviour in the world. As the Redemption was to take place by suffering and as our nature was to be raised up, it was necessary that a body should be prepared in order to be capable of suffering and in order to raise up our nature to its position before the Fall. Our first parents fell from their supernatural state, and to be raised up to that state again, it was necessary that this same nature should make good what it had destroyed. It had lost Sanctifying Grace, which means a participation in the Divine Nature, and only One possessing divine nature could again elevate this nature once more. Hence the necessity of God becoming man, or of what is known as the God-Man, now called Christ. The Second Divine Person of the Blessed Trinity took up a human nature, and by suffering He restored to mankind far more than ever we lost by the Fall of Adam and Eve. In reality, the Fall of our first parents gave the opportunity for the appearance of the God-Man, or Christ, through whom so many have reached great heights of glory. We need not spend much time worrying over the Fall of Adam and Eve because it has turned out in the goodness of God to be a great blessing for us.

The Fall of our first parents merely meant that they lost the supernatural state which is called the state of grace. This state of grace raises up our nature and makes us God-like or capable of enjoying the vision of God. It makes us partakers of the Divine Nature. Our natures have to be specially raised up by grace in order to be able to enjoy God for eternity. We may compare this with a blind man in this world. He cannot see the beauties of nature, nor can he enjoy those sights produced by art for the temporal happiness of the human race. The beauty of mountain, stream and lake has no meaning for him. In much the same way, our souls must be enlightened and receive the supernatural gifts in order to enjoy the beauties of Heaven or to be able to look on the eternal beauty of God.

Adam and Eve had lost this state of grace, and as they could not transmit to others what they did not possess themselves, so their children and descendants, as they appeared in this world, were also without this supernatural state, or without Sanctifying Grace. Who was then to be the Messias, or how could any child of Adam ever be able to redeem the world? How was he to be raised up from the fallen state? As the years passed on, the children of Adam realized the loss they sustained by the Fall, and hence arose numerous sighs and prayers from many holy souls for the coming of the Messias. At length God chooses one man, called Abraham, and sets him apart from the rest of the world. He asks Abraham to offer up sacrifices and promises that from his seed the Messias will appear. The prayers and sacrifices of Abraham were all intended to fit him to be the forefather of the Messias. From the time of Moses, God specified more and more the individual people and tribe and family from whom the Messias was to spring, and all the ceremonies and sacrifices of the Jews were a preparation for the Messias.

The prayers and sufferings of all the prophets and saints of the Old Law were all intended to gain grace to fit the world and to prepare one of the children of Adam to be the Mother of the Redeemer. At length, after thousands of years and after much prayer and suffering, both the world is prepared for the appearance of Christ and a woman is found at last worthy to be His Mother. It took all those prayers and sacrifices to obtain sufficient grace to prepare one soul to be the Mother of Christ. This is what is meant by the Immaculate Conception. Original Sin merely means the loss of grace. The Immaculate Conception means the restoration of grace once more to the human race. It does not mean that the prayers of the patriarchs earned the grace of the Immaculate Conception. This was brought about by all the prayers and sufferings of the saints of the Old Law, which were united to the future sufferings of Christ, and in this way this state of grace was restored once more to one child, who was the daughter of Joachim and Ann and of the tribe of David and a descendant of Abraham. Her name was called Mary, and she was after all those years found ready to be the Mother of the Redeemer, who was to restore not only what we lost by the Fall of Adam and Eve but in reality to give us graces and blessings by His sufferings, which are capable of raising us to the highest union with God.

The Immaculate Conception, then, was the long looked-for event in the history of the world, and from this we may really trace all the good things we have received through the sufferings and death of Christ. The Immaculate Conception means that, from the first moment of her existence, Mary was filled with Sanctifying Grace and was free from the supernatural effects of Original Sin. She was still liable to suffering, but this was really the means of her cooperation in the redemption of the world. We can understand now why Mary prefers this title to all other titles. It is a beautiful title to be called Mother of God, and Comforter of the Afflicted, or Queen of Heaven. But the foundation of all these titles is her Immaculate Conception, or the possession of God's grace. We can perhaps see now why Mary is honored so much and why she is associated with her Divine Son in all works for the salvation of souls. This explains really the power of her intercession. The efficacy of prayer depends upon the amount of grace we possess in our souls. Sanctifying grace raises us up and makes us partakers of the Divine Nature. Mary was elevated higher than all the saints put together, and hence her prayers are more powerful than those of all the saints combined. The more grace we have in our souls the more right we have to ask, and almost to demand, graces from God, because God has so raised us up as to make us like Himself and to give us much of His own power. This also explains the saying of the saints that all graces are given through Mary. She represents the human race, and those who will now make full use of the sufferings of Christ can appeal to Mary for grace because she has the right to be heard when she prays.

The Immaculate Conception also means that Mary was free from concupiscence or from the inclination to go to excess in the use of the faculties of nature. This freedom from concupiscence arose from the fullness of grace with which her soul was adorned. Some of the saints before their deaths also possessed practically this freedom from concupiscence because of the purity of their souls, or because of the amount of grace they had acquired by prayer and by the performance of supernatural good works. The lessons to be drawn from the reflections on the Immaculate Conception are very many, but they may all be reduced to an appreciation of the value of God's grace. We can become in some degree like unto Mary Immaculate by the preservation of the purity of our souls and by using every possible means to increase the state of Sanctifying Grace in our souls. One of the best means of doing so is to have a great devotion to Mary Immaculate and to guard above all things the angelic virtue of purity. Those who consecrate the purity of their souls to the Immaculate Virgin and offer the three Hail Marys morning and night in honor of the Immaculate Conception of Mary are making the best possible provision for the preservation of their purity. Like Mary we ought to aim at the possession of Sanctifying Grace and we should increase the state of graces in our souls by prayer, by receiving Holy Communion frequently and by the performance of works of self-denial.

> O purest of creatures, sweet Mother, sweet Maid,
> The one spotless womb wherein Jesus was laid,
> Dark night hath come down on us, Mother, and we
> Look out for thy shining, sweet Star of the Sea.

THE IMMACULATE CONCEPTION

THE NATIVITY OF MARY

CHAPTER II

The Nativity of Mary

ALTHOUGH we observe the holy season of Christmas as a time of joy on account of the birth of the Redeemer, yet the Feast of the Annunciation is really a more important and fundamental feast. Christmas was the visible appearance of Jesus, but the mystery of the Incarnation was really accomplished when the angel announced the glad tidings to Mary that she was to become the Mother of the Redeemer: "And the Word was made flesh and dwelt among us." It is somewhat different in the case of Our Lady, and we find that the feast of her Immaculate Conception now receives greater manifestations of joy and gladness than the feast of her Nativity. Before the birth of Jesus, the world had never witnessed such a day as the birth of Mary. As this child appears in the world on the 8th of September, the devils may not realize that their long-foretold defeat has arrived and that at last the woman has appeared who is destined to crush the head of the enemy of mankind.

The birth of Mary, like that of Jesus, was not marked by worldly wealth or grandeur. It was even more hidden than the birth of Jesus because Jesus was announced to the shepherds by the ministry of angels, but we hear of no such manifestation in the case of Mary. It is very probable that her parents, Joachim and Ann, were not blessed with worldly wealth because we never notice any great event for the salvation of souls built upon worldly grandeur or worldly power. Mary had wealth beyond that of all the kings of the world or all the strength of empires. In the eyes of God worldly wealth and power are of little consequence. The power of great empires

9

and great kingdoms will be of little value on the Last Day, and it will be found that all worldly grandeur and power were only hindrances to the acquisition of grace. We notice that God never blesses His dearest and chosen friends with abundance of worldly goods because this would only cause them to set their hearts on this world and on its glories and pleasures. We may conclude that Mary was not born amidst the luxury of wealth and power, but she possessed treasures far beyond anything that this world could ever possess. Many patriarchs and kings had come into this world before the birth of Mary, and many great events had taken place, but this was the day for which the prophets sighed and for which the patriarchs prayed for hundreds of years. This baby girl possesses within herself riches and blessings which far surpass that of the angels in Heaven. From the first moment of her conception she was free from the stain of Original Sin. This simply means that her soul was adorned with God's grace in view of her future merits and her future dignity of being the Mother of Jesus.

We may justly reflect on this child on the day of her birth. Her soul has been endowed with gifts and graces never before heard of since the dawn of creation. The soul of Eve before the Fall was certainly adorned with grace, but the beauty of the soul of Mary was as much superior to that of Eve as the sun surpasses the moon in splendor. The perfect understanding of Mary's intellect from her infancy was the delight of the Blessed Trinity and the wonder of the angels. Her acts of homage and adoration were so frequent that the state of grace in her soul was constantly being increased so that every moment of her existence she was becoming nearer and nearer to God. We have no reason to be astonished now at her power in Heaven once we realize that her state of grace was being increased every moment by her interior life.

The feast of the Nativity of Mary brings to our minds

the importance and the value of the interior life of grace. Mary was the greatest of God's creatures, and yet her birth was marked by no external manifestation of power. This hidden life of Mary was intended in the designs of Providence to teach to all future ages that what really matters in the sight of God is the interior life, or the life of grace in the soul. External honors and dignities are of no consequence in the sight of God unless the soul is closely united to God by the constant increase of Sanctifying Grace. Mary is really the model of all interior souls. These are the only souls in whom God takes special delight. Mary possessed all the charms and beauties with which nature could endow her. Her intellect was bright, deep, and beautiful, and she was specially enlightened by the Holy Ghost. She possessed a charm of personality by her maidenly dignity and her modesty of look and by the beauty of her countenance, which reflected as in a mirror the interior beauty of her soul. But all these qualities were not the cause of her greatness. The state of Sanctifying Grace in her soul was so great that she might almost be said to have had a faint knowledge of the Beatific Vision, even before she took her flight to God. The great lesson to be learned from the birth of Our Lady without any external grandeur is the importance of the possession of God's grace. The Immaculate Conception meant that the soul of Mary was filled with grace from the first moment of her existence.

Some may be inclined to say that we can learn very little from the graces possessed by Mary because her Immaculate Conception raises her above all others. It is true that the Immaculate Conception places Mary above all others, even including the angels, but we must remember that in Baptism our souls are cleansed from Original Sin and we are endowed with Sanctifying Grace. We must not expect that even after Baptism our souls are equal in grace to that of Mary, even before her birth, but yet we possess the foundation of the interior life of

Sanctifying Grace upon which we can build the super-structure of holiness. The cause of the loss of souls and the want of holiness is the want of appreciation of the value of Sanctifying Grace. The parents of Mary in every way cooperated with the designs of God in increasing the grace of this child of election.

What a pity that so many Christian parents, while they give some show of reverence for the gifts of the True Faith, yet by their conduct act as if grace and sin were of little consequence and that this world with its passing wealth and honors were the only thing that really mattered. We will notice parents sometimes who bewail the errors of their children and their ingratitude. These same children might say that the cause of their loss of grace was the evil influence of their home life. Oh, what a terrible account will not fathers and mothers have to render on the Judgment Day because, while they taught their children the Truth, yet by their lives and their example they undid much of the good of their teaching! How very few families do we find where the great concern is the seeking of God's grace? How many do we find who will seek after honors and worldly society and who will even risk the souls of their children for some worldly gain or for some worldly friendship?

If only the lives of parents would correspond more with the teachings of the Church, and if sin were regarded as the greatest evil in life, and grace the most important of all things, then the world would soon be turned into an earthly paradise. Our Blessed Lady, from the first day of her birth, made no account of the wealth and honors of the world. She had in view the acquiring of God's grace, and she wished to increase this by every action of her life. Oh, why are not the young taught the beauty of grace, and why are they not preserved in their Baptismal innocence? It may be objected that owing to the Fall of our first parents, human nature is inclined to evil and that the preservation of grace is difficult. This is one of those half-truths that have done so much to cause wrong views to be circulated. We have only, like Mary, to strengthen our souls by Sanctifying Grace, and we will be able quite easily to preserve our Baptismal innocence and to grow in grace by the performance of supernatural good works. Mary performed acts of adoration and prayed from her earliest existence.

The ordinary child, after Baptism, can be taught to pray to God as soon as it is able to speak. Whatever a child learns, even before it comes to the full use of reason, will be more lasting than what is learned at any other period of its life. In this way, the seeds of holiness sown in the earliest years will produce fruit when the child comes to maturity. It is such a pity that so many parents allow these years to pass by without profiting by them. Since the death of Our Lord, we now possess the greatest of treasures in the Blessed Eucharist. If children were early in life taught to nourish their souls with this Heavenly Food and if all through life they would continue to receive this Spiritual Food of their souls, they would receive strength to overcome all temptations, and they would, like Our Lady, grow in grace as they grow in years. Prayer and frequent reception of Holy Communion is all that is necessary to reach the greatest heights of sanctity. Everything else will follow from these, and once people begin to realize that the Holy Communion is as necessary for the health of the soul as ordinary food is for that of the body, then they will begin to acquire true sanctity and to cultivate the true interior life.

The birth of Mary brings to us the meaning of the interior life. Our external works are only of value in proportion to the state of grace in our souls or to our union with God. This is why the actions of some of the saints who never appeared in public but lived in the cloister or away from the tumult of the world were raised up to great heights of holiness. This arose from their interior life or their eagerness to increase the state of Sanctifying Grace in their soul. Mary led the interior life in all its activity and in all its beauty. She is really the model for all those who wish to acquire sanctity. Mary increased the state of Sanctifying Grace by her great purity of intention. Her whole life was spent in forgetfulness of self and in doing God's will. No child of Adam ever thought less of herself than Mary. Her thoughts were constantly occupied with God and she only thought of how she could give God glory.

When she was asked to become the Mother of the Redeemer, she said: "Behold the handmaid of the Lord." This purity of intention, or of doing every action to please God, made the most trivial actions of Mary meritorious. Mary was again in constant communication with God in prayer. This sanctified all her actions more and more and united her closer and closer to God. We can imitate Mary here at least by saying frequent aspirations and by offering each little action or each little sacrifice in union with the works and sufferings of Jesus and Mary for the salvation of souls. As a preparation for this feast let us offer our Holy Communion that we may obtain that purity of intention and that zeal for souls that characterized the whole life of Mary. If we consecrate to this tender Virgin our purity of soul, she will preserve it for us, and if we ask her to protect us from all the snares of the devil, she will shield us with her mantle. May this sweet Mother be more loved in the years to come, and she will then bring all her children to the feet of Jesus.

> Hail, Mary, Pearl of Grace,
>   Pure flower of Adam's race,
> And vessel rare of God's election;
>   Unstained as virgin snow,
> Serene as sunset's glow,
>   We sinners crave thy sure protection.

OUR LADY AND ST. ANN

THE PRESENTATION OF MARY IN THE TEMPLE

CHAPTER III

The Presentation of Mary in the Temple

WHEN the child Mary was three years old, she obtained permission from her parents to give herself up entirely to the service of God. She was received at this early age among the maidens consecrated to the Lord, and she lived in the Temple for twelve years. Her life in the Temple was so hidden that we know practically nothing about it, although St. John Damascene says that Mary in the Temple was occupied with the care of the little children who were in suffering or sickness and that she consoled them in their little troubles. Whenever a dispute arose, little Mary was sent for, and it is said that Mary was able to restore peace by her very presence. She made herself the servant of all and was prompt to perform acts of kindness to her little companions. Although the child Mary was weak in body like other children, her soul was so filled with grace that she really had no spiritual childhood. She was engaged from her earliest existence in making acts of adoration and love, and by these supernatural actions she was constantly growing in God's grace and in interior beauty.

This hidden life of Mary in the Temple teaches us the great secret of holiness. During the twelve years that Mary spent in the Temple, she did not suspect the great dignity to which she was one day to be raised. She merely wished to remain hidden from the world and to be known only to God. We see here the depth and beauty of Mary's intellect, even at this early age. She realized that all worldly honors are only passing and empty and so are not worthy of the consideration of a soul destined for the everlasting enjoyment of God. She had no desire for the companionship or the friendship of worldlings, nor did she set any value on the influence to be gained by the enjoyment of the patronage of the great people of the world. The beautiful and clear intellect of Mary was able to see at a glance that the friendship and protection of God is quite enough for us. She could understand quite clearly that we are well enough known when we are known to God and that we do quite enough if we do God's will. Mary realized that many poor foolish worldlings spend their time in external works and suffer many hardships and yet gain no happiness, either in time or in eternity, from all their labors. Instead of acquiring grace, these foolish people set their hearts on the passing things of this world and give their attention to pleasing people and to the acquisition of wealth and honors. Oh, the number of souls that are lost through this horrible desire to please people and to gain popularity! When will people begin to realize and to act upon the knowledge that we do quite enough when we please God, and that we are well enough known and have quite enough friends if we are known to God and if we enjoy God's friendship?

Mary was destined for the most sublime of all vocations; therefore, God enticed Mary into solitude in order to prepare her for her great vocation. "I will lead her into solitude, and there I will speak to her heart," says the Holy Ghost, the Spouse of Mary. It is only in solitude that we can hear the whisperings of the Holy Spirit. In the noise and bustle of the world our thoughts are taken up too much with exterior things to allow the Holy Ghost to enlighten us or to give us His sweet inspirations. Mary's heart was so free from all worldly desires that the Holy Ghost found her capable of receiving every inspiration, and as Mary corresponded with every good thought, she grew to such a degree of holiness that the Angel Gabriel declared her full of grace and St. Elizabeth was astonished that one so exalted should condescend to visit her home.

When we hear of souls being raised to great heights of sanctity or when they do unique things for God's glory, we may always conclude that the seeds of holiness were sown and were allowed to germinate in solitude. If the ground into which the seeds are deposited is too often disturbed, we cannot expect the seeds to germinate. The seed must be hidden in the earth for a considerable time before the trees appear. If we expect the fruits too soon or if we force the plants to yield their fruits before the appointed time, then we only end by damaging the whole tree, and its fruits will not be lasting. It is much the same in the case of souls. If we wish to increase in grace, we must hide from the eyes of the world and live in solitude where the Holy Ghost Himself will prepare us for our future works, for our own sanctification and God's glory. We learn also from the hidden life of Mary the value of silence concerning the graces with which we are endowed by God.

Mary did not suspect at this early age her great vocation, but by her desire to remain hidden and by her silence concerning the graces with which God had endowed her she proved herself worthy of being the confidant of God in the most momentous decisions concerning the redemption of the world. Mary kept all God's secrets, and thus she never was able to be despoiled of any grace, although the devils must have longed to know what was in store for this youthful maiden. This is a great lesson for those who are called by God to any special vocation. How many vocations are spoiled by the devil simply because silence was not observed in the early stages of the development of the spiritual life. The devil uses others to crush vocations in their infancy as soon as the vocation is made public. Mary allowed her vocation to develop hidden from the public gaze and so it was saved from the wiles of Satan. In the performance of a good work it is also necessary to keep secrecy until the seeds sown have sufficient time to germinate. After this the biting blasts of criticism and jealousy will not be able to destroy it because it has taken deep root and its branches are spread in all directions.

We may learn another great lesson from the life of Mary in the Temple. This hidden life of Mary was not an idle or useless existence. She was continually growing in grace by her fidelity to God's inspirations and by the performance of supernatural good works. Our great object in life ought to be to increase the state of Sanctifying Grace in our souls. This is done by the performance of good works for a supernatural end, and while our souls are already in the state of grace. Some perform many good actions and yet gain no everlasting reward because their souls are not in the state of grace and because their intentions are not supernatural. We could so easily become saints, because all sanctity consists in the degree of union with God, which corresponds exactly with the amount of grace in the soul. We have only to perform every action simply to please God.

Some are kept from sanctity through scruples. This is one of the cleverest tricks of the devil to keep a soul from reaching exceptional heights of holiness. Mary was never scrupulous, because her intellect was so clear that she could judge correctly on the value of her acts in the sight of God. Mary's simplicity saved her from the snares of scrupulosity, which the devil lays for generous souls. By simplicity we do not mean stupidity or dullness of intellect. Simplicity means to be straight and honest in all our actions and intentions. Mary was simple in the supernatural sense that she sought God in all her actions. Mary observed the commandments with a perfection unequalled by any child of Adam, and her soul was never sullied by the least stain of sin. But in all her actions she only thought of pleasing God—in much the same way as a fond child will please its sweet and loving mother.

THE CHILD MARY AT PRAYER

Muller

THE ANNUNCIATION

CHAPTER IV

The Annunciation
The Beautiful Intellect of Mary

IN viewing the personality of Our Lady, what first strikes us is her wonderfully developed mind and her quickness of intelligence. When the Archangel Gabriel appears to her and announces that she has been chosen to be the Mother of the Redeemer, she received the heavenly messenger with a calmness and a delicacy which must even have surprised the angel himself. When the angel announced to her the glad tidings, she did not at once accept or refuse, but with simplicity and freedom she asked how this could be accomplished in view of her vow of virginity. This request for information about her vow shows her great interior liberty of spirit and her freedom from all self seeking or vainglory. What a beautiful mind must this young maiden had to have to think of asking this question.

Some have taught that Mary at first refused the dignity of being the Mother of God on account of her vow. This teaching is certainly not showing sufficient acknowledgment of Our Lady's greatness of mind. To have refused to perform the will of God in order to preserve her vow (because even a vow no longer binds when there is a question of doing something better), would at once have marked Our Lady as being a mediocrity. Our Lady took in the whole situation and merely asked the question about her vow. She had not the least intention of refusing to cooperate in the salvation of the world. As soon as the angel assured her that her vow would still be preserved and that the Holy Ghost would operate, she simply answers, ''Behold the handmaid of the Lord: Be it done unto me according to thy word." These words merely meant that Mary was ready to be used as it pleased God to use her. Previous to this, Mary had offered herself to God. Now, when the time came for God to accept her offering, she was ready for the sacrifice. She was inspired to vow her virginity to God because God wished to preserve her for the Divine motherhood, and when the time came to make the great sacrifice, she did not withdraw what was previously offered. Oh, how many souls in the fervor of their love for God during periods of grace and recollection offer themselves to God and promise very much for the welfare of souls—but take back later all their early promises, or when the sacrifice is really asked, they give it with such reluctance that God scarcely accepts their half-hearted offering! Mary knew that the work of Redemption could only be accomplished by suffering, but yet she makes no condition with the angel and asks for no signs of his credentials, nor does she in any way limit her sacrifice.

The Mystery of the Annunciation shows Mary in her sweetness and greatness. All sanctity consists in forgetfulness of self and in generosity with God and souls. Sanctity also means perfect trust and confidence in God, just as the little child in the arms of its mother has unlimited trust and asks no questions about the future, so long as it nestles on the bosom of its fond parent. Mary asked no questions about her future sufferings or her future glory. God's will was made known to her, and she asks nothing more. We here again see the beautiful intellect of Our Lady. Surely we do quite enough if we do God's will. What need have we for anxiety for the future if we keep close to God? What should we care about glory or honor if we are in the friendship of God? Oh, how deep was the intelligence of Mary! She suffers no elation at her future glory, nor does she ask any questions about her humiliations nor the details of the works of Redemption. To have done so would have been to gratify curiosity, and Mary had no desire for anything but to promote God's interest. To have felt, or rather to have given way to feelings of elation or vanity, would have shown emptiness of mind and absence of grace. Human applause gave Mary no concern. She could realize that human glory was passing and fickle, but Heavenly glory, or the grace of God, was lasting and certain. Mary realized that great things had been done by the grace or by the power of God and that she was only chosen as the instrument in carrying out the works of salvation. We never see a truly humble soul that is not at the same time possessed of a deep intelligence and a sound judgment. Humility is only another name for truth, and it requires a strong intellect to grasp truth in all its bearings and all its causes and consequences. Mary realized that all her gifts came from God and that all her human glory was not intended for the gaining of the passing applause of this world, but for the much greater and essential work of bringing souls to the everlasting rewards of Heaven.

The angel announces to Mary that her cousin, St. Elizabeth, had conceived. This news, that Elizabeth in her advanced years had been blessed with motherhood, immediately stirred the heart of the humble virgin to sentiments of joy. In the ordinary course of events, it might be thought that as Mary was now raised to the dignity above all dignities, of being selected for the office of the Mother of the long-expected Messias, she would no longer perform the ordinary humble duties suitable to her rank. But the deep and beautiful intellect of Mary again rises to the occasion, and she hastens to visit her cousin. When Mary arrived at the house of Zachary, Elizabeth, filled with admiration and humility, said, ''Why is it that the Mother of My Lord should visit me?'' Elizabeth marvelled at the humility of Mary in visiting her after she had been selected for such a dignity. At that moment the infant in the womb of Elizabeth leapt for joy because he was there and then sanctified by the presence of Mary and the Divine Infant which she carried within her. The beautiful mind of Mary was able to realize that the performance of works of charity and kindness was in no way incompatible with the highest heavenly honors.

Mary, moreover, realized as very few realize that all honors and dignities carry with them great responsibility and that those who abuse any of God's gifts will have to render an account of it on the great day of Judgment. It is such a misfortune for the Church and for souls to find some who hold positions of authority using their positions and their gifts for selfish ends and to gratify vanity or pride. Mary received the highest of all offices, but never once in her life did she ever think of herself or of her own reward in the discharge of her duties. She had only one thought all through her life: "Behold the handmaid of the Lord, be it done unto me according to thy word." It was for her simply a matter of doing God's will. Mary is an example—especially to parents and those in authority—of disinterested love in the service of God.

In the house of Elizabeth, Mary utters the famous prayer or psalm called the "Magnificat," which is the evening prayer of the Church, in her official prayer of Vespers. This beautiful canticle of praise expresses the sentiments of Our Lady's heart at the joys of her Divine maternity and indicates the superiority of her mind. She says that her soul magnifies the Lord and her spirit rejoices in God her Saviour because He has regarded the lowliness of His handmaid and from henceforth all generations would call her blessed. She gives here the chief reason for her having been chosen to be the Mother of Jesus. She was chosen chiefly on account of her lowliness or her humility. In other words, she says that she was lowly or little in the eyes of the world, and so God raised her up by His grace and fitted her for this dignity and this exalted office.

We have here some food for reflection. The humility or lowliness of Mary meant that she neither was great nor did she desire greatness in the eyes of the world. Here again we see the superiority of Mary's intellect, aided of course by God's grace. From her earliest years she had vowed her virginity to God. She was content to remain hidden from the eyes of the world, and for this generosity God gave her the highest of all spiritual blessings. Mary humbled herself so much that she forgot herself entirely and only wished to live for and to love God, and so she was exalted. Our Lord Himself said during His Public Life that those who humbled themselves would be exalted, and we see this all through the economy of grace and salvation. Whatever sacrifices we make for Our Lord (and all sacrifice means some self-denial or self-forgetfulness) will be rewarded a hundred fold in spiritual blessings, and we will gain as well the eternal years of glory. Mary was raised up because she fitted herself for this exaltation by her absolute indifference to all worldly honors or all dignities. She merely thought of God's honor and glory, and God is never outdone or surpassed in generosity.

Mary in this canticle further says that God has done great things to her. Here again we see her humility, which is merely the love of truth. Had Mary said that she had not received great graces from God, she would not have really been humble. She attributes all her gifts to God and takes no credit for anything herself. This is the real proof of humility: Give all glory to God from whom are all good things. Some may perhaps be inclined to ask why Mary uttered this canticle, which made known her gifts and graces. Mary had no desire to make known what gifts God had bestowed upon her, but when her cousin St. Elizabeth manifested her sentiments of admiration at the humility of the Mother of God in condescending to visit her, Mary answers in this canticle that all glory and thanks are due to God alone from whom all her graces came. During the rest of her life, we never hear of Mary so much as mentioning the gifts that God bestowed upon her, and even to St. Joseph she did not reveal the words of the angel. We again see the humility and the deep intelligence of Mary. She was too prudent to divulge God's secret to anybody. She realized that her duty was to be the Mother of Jesus and to protect her Child, but the manifestation of the coming of the Redeemer did not enter into her vocation, and so she wisely kept silent. Had she made it known she might easily have aroused the jealousy of Herod or the Pharisees.

Gagliardi

THE ANNUNCIATION

Gagliardi

THE ADORATION OF THE SHEPHERDS

CHAPTER V

The First Christmas Night

I N viewing the sorrows of Mary, we will find that each dolor or each cross was a preparation for some great grace and that her greatest sorrows preceded the final years of her life, which were a foretaste of the eternal years of glory. It is the universal law of the spiritual or, to be more accurate, of the supernatural life, that every grace must be purchased at the price of sacrifice. The sufferings may be very short and may pass very quickly, but the rewards will be everlasting and will exceed any happiness that could even be conceived by the human mind.

In considering the dolors of Mary, we generally bring them under seven heads, or rather we concentrate our attention on the seven chief sorrows of her life. We usually begin with the prophecy of holy Simeon, who made known to her that the sword of sorrow would pierce her heart. This was not really the beginning of her sorrows. On the first Christmas night, Mary underwent with her spouse, St. Joseph, great anguish of mind. The command of Caesar insisted that all the people should be enrolled in the tribal city of each family. This taking of the Roman census was permitted by God to fulfill many prophecies and to work out the designs of Divine Providence. It was intended in the first place to fulfill the prophecy that Christ would be born in Bethlehem, as foretold by the prophet Micheas, and the enrollment in the Roman records was proof sufficient that the scepter had passed away from Juda, which was foretold by the prophet Daniel. The journey from Nazareth to Bethlehem was also an occasion of merit on the part of Our Lady and St. Joseph, and the inconveniences of the journey and their resignation to God's will under trying circumstances were the means used by God to sanctify them for the stupendous grace of the birth of the Redeemer. The world was to receive the great grace of the long-expected Messias, and Mary was to be the chief instrument in bringing the Saviour to the world. This unique grace, like all other graces, had to be purchased by suffering; hence, we now understand the poverty of the manger and the desolation of Mary and St. Joseph on the first Christmas night when they could find no place to rest and were repulsed at all the inns of Bethlehem.

We must first realize that Mary bore Jesus the entire time of her anxiety on the first Christmas night, and yet it would seem as if she were altogether abandoned by God. St. Joseph and Our Lady on leaving Nazareth never thought they would meet with such sorrow or distress nor be left altogether so desolate. They trusted to Divine Providence, but it would seem as if God had altogether forgotten them. They go from door to door seeking for shelter, but the inns or lodging houses were filled, and there was no room for them. In Bethlehem on that night many wealthy and important people had come from various parts of Judea and Galilee and had found hospitality in the various homes built by Herod, but still there is no room for Mary and her spouse St. Joseph.

They knocked at many a door, but just as surely were they repulsed. They seemed to be the most desolate and worthless of all God's creatures, but every anxiety and every humiliation was intended for their sanctification, and not one act of sorrow or one act of rudeness inflicted upon them was unrecorded or unrewarded by God. They quietly bore with all their sorrows and humiliations, and they excused all the insults and unkindness to which they were subjected. They go outside the little town of Bethlehem, and there they find a cave, or a sort of stable, for oxen. And here they enter, having to accept this as a resting place, and in this stable the long-expected

Redeemer of the world was born. This was the first meeting with the world which Jesus had, and at His birth the world had rejected Him. It did not want Him. Mary and Joseph were the chosen souls hidden and unknown in the world who were the link between Heaven and earth. The world has never had any time for Christ and never will have, nor will it ever have any time for the friends of Christ. Those who wish to follow Jesus and cooperate with Him in the salvation of souls need never expect to be welcomed in worldly society. They must expect to be repulsed like Mary and St. Joseph on the first Christmas night, but just like the Holy Family, they are not forgotten by God, although they may seem to be left without assistance. Their sorrows are all intended for their sanctification and to make them worthy instruments in the salvation of souls. The saints have never been popular with the world.

The manger at Bethlehem is a subject for long and profitable meditation. The Holy Family here find a resting place, and here the Saviour of the human race finds His first abode in this world. The Evangelist records that Mary wrapped the Infant in swaddling bands and laid Him in a manger. The angels appear to the poor shepherds singing songs of joy, but there seems little reason for joy at the poverty of the manger and at the swaddling bands and the straw. The barest necessaries only are provided for Jesus, and the only adorers or companions at the birth of Jesus were the poor shepherds and Our Lady and St. Joseph. Jesus had well prepared His Holy Mother to be a mother of the poor and the afflicted. How she rejoiced when even the poor shepherds came to offer their homage to her newborn Babe. She had borne with sorrow and anxiety and had felt the world's neglect on account of her poverty and so she sympathized with the poor, simple shepherds on the first Christmas night. We may not wonder to find the friends of Mary in all ages among the poor and the humble. At Lourdes she chose a little shepherdess to be the bearer of a message to the world. She chooses, even to found institutions for the benefit of the poor and for the salvation of souls, those who are not great in the eyes of the world. She can always look back to the first Christmas night, and she remembers that the great and the wealthy had no time for her, nor for her Divine Son. Only the poor, hard-working shepherds took time to pay a visit to the humble manger on that night. Others would have been scandalized at the poverty of the manger, and they would never have adored a God born into this world in such destitution. Ever since the first Christmas, the world and its followers have had no time for Jesus and even less time for Mary. She still has to choose from the ranks of the poor and the simple those who are to cooperate in carrying on good works for the salvation of souls, and even now many among the children of the Church are ashamed to be associated with those simple and humble souls on account of their poverty and obscurity. Mary gives to the poor shepherds her Divine Son to caress, and these poor men take the Infant in their arms, and the heart of the Mother is consoled because even a few people pay some respect and give some tokens of gratitude to her little Child Jesus.

From the manger we may draw the very profitable lesson that those who are generally God's dearest friends are the poor and humble. On the first Christmas night, the world and those who followed the world in their pursuit of its wealth and honors had no time for Jesus nor Mary. The world was sufficient for them. The poor shepherds had little of the goods of this world, but they were worthy of a special message from Heaven which was made known to them through angels. They were not so engrossed in the affairs of the world as to have no time for Jesus nor for the affairs of eternity. The only pity is that so many in this world have to suffer from poverty and want, but they carry their crosses with so much reluctance that they murmur against God and so lose most of the merit of their sufferings. Even the friends of God who may be engaged in good works for the salvation of souls will often be found to rebel against opposition and obstacles placed in their way, instead of sanctifying themselves by prayer and patience and by offering all their sacrifices to the Sacred Heart of Jesus for the salvation of souls. When souls are filled with sorrow and when God seems to have abandoned them, they will then prove their love and confidence by still trusting to the goodness of God.

The Holy Family had to seek for shelter in a cave or in a habitation used only for the beasts of the field. Everything is so unprepared and everything looks so inhospitable. Yet Mary and St. Joseph make no complaint about their poverty because they have Jesus. Our Lord Himself makes no complaint about the poverty of the manger nor the absence of human grandeur because He has a few loving hearts to give Him a welcome. As Our Lady gave the sweet Infant to the poor shepherds on that night and as their humble efforts to show their homage to Jesus and their congratulations to Mary pleased the Mother of the Saviour, so will we console both Jesus and Mary for the ingratitude of the first Christmas night if we will give Jesus a welcome within our souls in Holy Communion. Jesus is not anxious for great buildings, and if He lives in beautiful churches, it is only to show His appreciation of the sacrifices we offer in making a home for Him, but the home that Jesus truly wishes is in the hearts of His faithful children in Holy Communion. He wishes only to give us graces to sanctify us for the eternal joys of Paradise. From the poverty of the manger we can also learn of the worthlessness of worldly goods and of worldly pomp. What a pity that so many give their hearts to the amassing of wealth instead of amassing the grace of God for eternity! What a pity that people will not trust more in Divine Providence and in times of sorrow and distress not give way to murmurings but sanctify themselves by resignation to God's will! Mary seemed to be entirely forgotten by God on the first Christmas night, but angels were guarding her every step, and the sorrows and disappointments were all required to increase her sanctity and her eternal glory and to increase her sympathy and her kindness for the poor and the suffering in this world.

> Mother of Christ, Mother of Christ,
>   What shall I ask of thee?
> I do not sigh for the wealth of earth,
>   For the joys that fade and flee;
>
> But Mother of Christ, Mother of Christ,
>   This do I long to see,
> The Bliss untold which thine arms enfold,
>   The Treasure upon thy knee.
>
> Mother of Christ, Mother of Christ,
>   He was All-in-all to thee
> In the winter's cave, in Nazareth's home,
>   In the hamlets of Galilee.
>
> So Mother of Christ, Mother of Christ
>   He will not say nay to thee;
> When He lifts His face to thy sweet embrace,
>   Speak to Him, Mother of me.

THE ADORATION OF THE MAGI

Janssens

THE FIRST SORROW—THE PROPHECY OF SIMEON

CHAPTER VI

The Prophecy of Holy Simeon

THE Presentation, or the feast of Purification, took place forty days after the birth of Jesus on Christmas night, and Our Lady fulfilled all the prescriptions of the Old Law by presenting herself for the ceremony of purification, although she was not really bound by the law, as the birth of Jesus was a virginal one. She wished to give good example and to avoid even the least semblance of scandal. This was also an act of humility on the part of Our Lady, and it was the wish of God also because the virginal conception of Jesus was not known to the world. On this occasion, Jesus is presented to His Heavenly Father for the first time, and the ceremony takes place in the Temple at Jerusalem.

As the Holy Family approach the Temple, the holy old man Simeon, enlightened by the Holy Ghost, recognizes the Infant as the long-promised and long-expected Messias or Redeemer. Holy Simeon then utters the famous prayer called the *Nunc Dimittis*, or evening prayer, which the Church uses in her official prayer every evening. The holy old man said that he was now prepared to leave this world as his eyes had rested on the Saviour and he had nothing more to live for. He utters the famous prophecy concerning Jesus and Mary: "Behold this Child is set for the fall and for the resurrection of many in Israel, and for a sign which shall be contradicted: And thine own soul a sword shall pierce." Holy Simeon here reveals the future life and contradictions of Jesus and the piercing sorrows of Mary, and this prophecy cast its shadows over the heart of Mary for the following thirty-three years, or until she received the dead body of Jesus in her arms. Little wonder she did not appear during the glories of Jesus, when He was working His greatest

39

miracles, or with the crowd on Palm Sunday. She knew from the prophecy of holy Simeon that all these glories would give place to humiliations and that she herself would have to suffer with Jesus and thus cooperate in the work of Redemption.

Each word uttered by holy Simeon was like a sword passing through her heart, and we must feel sympathy for this young and tender maiden, whose soul was as spotless as the snow and whose heart was as tender as any mother's heart could be, being told that she was to bear terrible sorrows. She was still young in years and had not witnessed much of the sorrows of the world, except those of Christmas night when she was refused admittance to all the inns in Bethlehem. She had given her consent to be the Mother of the Saviour, and she must even then have known that the Redemption would be accomplished by suffering and sorrow, but now some of the details of her future sufferings are revealed to her. Her Son was to be set up as a sign of contradiction. How these words of Simeon caused anguish and disappointment to the sweet and tender heart of Mary!

No mother ever loved her child as Mary loved her Infant, and she pressed Him to her bosom in accents of love and in the maternal affections of her virginal heart. She was joyous at the birth of Jesus because she looked forward to the redemption of her people of Israel and to the subsequent salvation of all the kingdoms of the earth. She had borne anguish of mind on the night of the birth of Jesus, but since she set her maternal eyes on the divine Infant and looked forward to all the souls saved by Him, she had been filled with joy. Now her joy is suddenly changed to unspeakable anguish and disappointment. Her kind heart looked forward to the saving of all the souls in the world, and she did not mind so much the sufferings to be undergone by herself or by Jesus so long as salvation was promised to mankind and Jesus was honored and adored by all the people for their own salvation. She receives a terrible shock when she hears the holy old man saying that her Son is set up for the ruin of many and for a sign of contradiction. Her Son set up for the ruin of many, and she is His Mother! Oh, what a feeling of disappointment and desolation passed through the heart of this tender Virgin at the thought of Jesus being the ruin of many!

She may not fully have realized the meaning of the words or how her Son was to be a sign of contradiction. Jesus is a sign of contradiction to those who will not accept His blessings or to those who plot for His destruction and for the overthrow of His Church. He is set up for the ruin of those who will not pay heed to His doctrines or make use of His graces. This prophecy means that no one can be indifferent with regard to Christ. He must be either loved or hated, and those who reach salvation are saved through faith in Christ and by the graces He gained for us by His Passion. Those who are lost incur damnation by rejecting Christ or by refusing His blessings. Christ is the only means of salvation, and if we do not make use of the blessings of Christ, we cannot reach our eternal reward. But Mary had never before realized that so many would be lost or would refuse the gifts of her sweet Babe.

The thought of Jesus being a sign of contradiction and the prophecy that many would be lost by their opposition to Jesus was the keenest disappointment that had ever yet crossed her path, and it destroyed for the future her girlish happiness. Henceforth, life held for her many serious problems, and from that Presentation in the Temple Mary wore a sweet sadness on her countenance which manifested the interior desolation of her soul. During the thirty years at Nazareth, amidst the joys of sweet domestic duties of the Holy Family, Mary could no longer give way to any joyous expression, and in moments of peace and quietness her maternal heart often gave vent to its sadness in heartfelt tears of sorrow and pity. The words of holy Simeon had left an impression upon her that cast its shadow over her whole life.

This first great sorrow of Mary had initiated the sweet Mother early in life into the mystery of suffering. During our lives we may sometimes see a young mother who has lost her only child, and this great sorrow makes an indelible impression on her for the rest of her life. We sometimes hear the wailing as of despair and as if all happiness has gone forever. Yet time heals such sorrows, and consolations in other ways are generally received by those who meet with great crosses in this world. With Mary it was a question of grief being increased as the days go by and of the withdrawal of all consolation. Each day brings more clearly before her mind the future sufferings of Jesus, and she reflects more and more on the loss of souls and the contradictions Jesus will meet with. Poor dear Mother Mary had early to bear the Cross. Her sweet smile and her kindness at the marriage feast at Cana were scarcely able to conceal the perpetual anguish of her soul. And Jesus gives her no comfort and no relief. She has to bear the anguish of the exile into Egypt and the desolation of the three days' loss, and Jesus during His life gives her no consolation because He wished to sanctify her and enable her to gain graces so as to cooperate by her prayers and sufferings in the salvation of souls. Jesus loved Mary as no son ever loved a mother, and yet He allows her to spend her years carrying her cross without alleviation, simply because He loved her so much and did not wish to deprive her of any degree of merit.

How many lessons may we draw from the consideration of this first dolor of Mary! Very few in the world are exempt from suffering, and some begin early to carry the Cross and are not free from it for the remainder of their lives. Some whom Jesus loves specially and whom He wishes to sanctify for great works for souls receive a heavy cross, which casts a gloom over their whole lives.

Unfortunately some carry their crosses with such reluctance that they gain nothing by all their sufferings. Others happily make use of their crosses to take their hearts away from the passing and empty joys of this world and center all their thoughts and affections on Jesus and on the acquisition of God's grace.

Sacrifice purifies the soul and gives an outlook on life's duties which raises the mind to lofty ideals and makes us capable of sympathizing with suffering and of making sacrifices for God and souls. Jesus during the thirty years at Nazareth could see His Holy Mother bearing her cross patiently, and He rejoiced to see her growing daily in sweetness and holiness. How often do we see people who possess the good things of the world becoming proud and arrogant and having no sympathy for the poor and the suffering. How often again do we see some soul purified by suffering, leading a life of holiness and sweetness and shedding brightness all around by her sweetness and kindness to all who approach her. Mary grew in holiness as she grew in age and she also grew in sweetness and kindness.

The Heart of Jesus rejoiced to see His Holy Mother growing in all graces and in all virtues, but especially in kindness. Jesus looked forward to the eternal years, and He saw all the souls saved by the charity and prayers of Mary, and so He left her without consolation that she might become more holy and more sympathetic and more charitable to the poor and to the sinner. How she sorrowed all those years over the fate of sinners who would be lost because they would reject Jesus! These years of sorrow have made Mary the hope of the afflicted and the refuge of sinners. Her love for Jesus and for souls grew every day of her life, and her occupation till the End of the World will be to bring souls to Jesus.

In our sorrows we ought to imitate Mary and bear them patiently for the love of Jesus and for the salvation of souls. Sorrow will purify us and make us more sympathetic and will enable us to gain very much for eternity. They will increase our love for Jesus and for souls and make us like the Mother of Sorrows. May she aid us to bear patiently all the crosses and trials of life.

Let us in all our trials and tribulations cling to Our Lord's holy will and, like Our Blessed Lady, be resigned and say:

> All for Thee, O Heart of Jesus,
>   All for Thee eternally;
> Nought for me, O Heart of Jesus,
>   Save to be beloved by Thee.
>
> Thou hast taught me in my sorrow
>   Where the heart alone finds rest;
> I have learned 'tis sweet to suffer,
>   pillowed on Thy Sacred Breast.
>
> Take from me, O Heart of Jesus,
>   All that holds me back from Thee,
> Was the prayer I long since whispered;
>   Well, full well, Thou'st answered me.
>
> Every hope once fondly cherished
>   One by one I've seen depart,
> Then earth had for me no sunshine,
>   Save alone Thy Sacred Heart.

THE PRESENTATION OF JESUS IN THE TEMPLE

Janssens

THE SECOND SORROW—THE FLIGHT INTO EGYPT

CHAPTER VII

The Flight into Egypt

OUR Blessed Lady was soon made to realize the truth spoken by holy Simeon, and the fulfillment of the prophetic words of the holy old man was not long delayed. The second great dolor or sorrow of Our Lady was caused by the wild passion of Herod, who ordered the massacre of all the infants around Bethlehem. An angel appears to Joseph in sleep, saying, "Arise and take the child and his mother, and fly into Egypt, and be there until I shall tell thee." This was a very hard command, and it would seem that poor St. Joseph was to have neither peace nor rest since Our Saviour appeared. St. Joseph was commanded to take the Child and His Mother and to make haste, for Herod sought to take the life of the Child. The journey to Egypt was a long and painful one and probably occupied seven or eight days. The way led through the desert over which the Israelites had come on their journey to the Promised Land. God provided a pillar of cloud to guide the Israelites and sent them manna and the miraculous water, but we have no account of any such prodigies being performed for the sake of the Holy Family. They were spared none of the inconveniences of the journey, and the good St. Joseph must have had great anxiety of mind to provide protection and support for the Mother and Child.

This flight into a strange country, and so hurriedly, was a cause of sorrow and suffering to Mary. The Baby Jesus was her greatest treasure, and she had the duty of protecting Him. As she pressed her sweet Babe to her breast through the desolate desert on the way to Egypt, she had many a silent heartache and many hours of anxiety and desolation. They had to leave in haste; no provision was made for the necessities of the journey, and no arrangements were made for their arrival. Mary and Joseph with the Infant seem to be the most deserted of all creatures, and no one appears to have any care for them. Mary has to care for Jesus, and every moment she is in fear of robbers and in fear of the pangs of hunger and want. Mary did not mind her own sufferings nor even losing her own life if it were God's will to take it by violent death, but her mission was to protect Jesus and bring Him up in such a way that He might be capable of carrying out the work of Redemption.

Very few realize the weight of this responsibility of protecting Jesus. What if she should fail! What if the work of Redemption were spoiled through her neglect of duty! She can lean upon St. Joseph for protection, but hers was the chief duty of the protection of Jesus. This responsibility for one so young and so inexperienced in the ways of the world was a cause of perpetual anxiety to the tender heart of Mary. Here it was the cruel Herod who was the cause of her sorrow, but in the goodness of her heart she does not wish for the destruction of Herod, nor does she complain of the exile nor of their poverty and distress. She minds no suffering if she can only save her Child for the salvation of the world. In Egypt the Holy Family may have met some Jewish families and may even have had friends among the Gentiles, and it is likely that God, as a reward for their obedience in going into exile, may have given them some consolations in this strange land, which had at one time been the home of the Israelites and of their great deliverer, Moses.

This flight into Egypt was caused by Herod, but God wished to teach a lesson and to give an example to all those who may have to suffer exile for their faith or for the love of God. Mary and Joseph here are the first foreign missioners, and they are the first to bring Jesus to the lands that are in darkness. How many have received courage from the thought of the flight of Mary and Joseph into Egypt to make the great sacrifice of leaving home and country to carry the good tidings of the Gospel to the poor heathen. It will be noticed that God generally asks His friends who go to preach the Gospel to make many sacrifices and to work for the glory of Jesus amidst trials and disappointments. What a source of consolation to remember the sacrifices of the Holy Family in their flight.

They rise up and make no provision because God has commanded them to go in haste. Yet God did not forget the Holy Family on their journey nor on their arrival. He left them without any apparent heavenly protection, but legions of angels were watching their every step and making provision for them by inducing others to show them kindness. It is just the same with those who make sacrifices for God: They may perhaps have to suffer anxiety, and it sometimes seems as if God had forgotten them. Yet, like the Holy Family, every anxiety and care is cherished and recorded by angels and these sorrows are all intended for their purification and sanctification and to fit them to carry on works for the salvation of souls.

In all the sorrows and anxieties of the flight, Mary still had one source of consolation—she still possessed Jesus. She was in danger of losing Him from the cruelty of wicked men, and this fear of the loss of Jesus gave her no peace, day or night during the journey. She clasped Jesus to her maternal heart, and every time she did so, her love grew stronger and more tender, and her heart was filled with the most unselfish love for Jesus and for souls. In the midst of all the desolation of the desert, Mary had also the supernatural peace which comes from the possession of Jesus. So long as Jesus was with her, she could not be deprived of this peace of soul, although at the same time she suffered agonies of mind and mental tortures. Mary suffered that she might so sanctify herself for her future work and that she might become later on the "Comforter of the Afflicted." In all our sorrows and disappointments, if we will only keep close to Jesus, like Mary in the flight into Egypt, we will always at least enjoy the assurance of God's friendship and gain great graces for eternity. Jesus knew of every anxiety of His Holy Mother, and yet He allows her to suffer in order to sanctify her. He wishes here to teach a lesson to all the faithful, but more especially to His own dear friends.

In all trials and sorrows, if we will only cling close to Jesus and bear the Cross with patience, we will gain wonderful graces for the future, and prepare ourselves for reaching a great height of glory. It is such a pity that so many lose most of the merit of their sufferings because they will not pray for grace. The saints became so holy simply on account of their close union with Jesus and because they offered their crosses in union with the sufferings of Jesus and Mary for the salvation of souls. What have we to fear so long as we have Jesus? Some may here say that Mary carried Jesus in her arms and so she was privileged beyond others. This is only partly true. She carried Jesus in her arms, but we can always have this same Jesus in our souls in Holy Communion, and we can converse with Him while we kneel before the tabernacle. Jesus rested on the sweet heart of Mary and in her arms on the way to Egypt, and as He rejoiced at the nobility and generosity of the heart of His Mother, so will He rejoice to make our hearts pure and holy if we will only allow Him to do so. He says, "My child, give Me thy heart." He sends us these little crosses and contradictions occasionally to sanctify us because He knows what is best for us. Oh, if we would only unite our little sufferings with those of Jesus and Mary and offer them to Jesus for the conversion of sinners, what a store of merit we would lay up for the eternal years and what graces we would obtain for the salvation of others! By the patience and by the very presence of Mary in Egypt many graces were given to that land, as we can see from the numbers of saints who flourished there in the early ages of the Church.

This dolor of Mary is also intended to teach the lesson of vocation. When it is God's will that we should make any sacrifice, then we will prove our love for God if we will do God's will and seek not for the reason of the command. The Holy Family were commanded to go into Egypt, and they simply obeyed. In this obedience they sanctified themselves more and more and became by their sufferings much nearer to God. Mary and Joseph had Jesus with them on the journey, but after having borne this cross, their souls were much more pleasing to God, and Jesus was much nearer to them. This is what takes place in the work of sanctification. Jesus sends us a cross in order to give us some special grace. Oh, if we would only accept these little crosses for the sake of Jesus, what graces and what interior peace of soul would be enjoyed afterwards! When Jesus asks a soul to make a sacrifice of leaving home or country for His sake, He never asks her to go alone. He is always there before her in the Holy Eucharist. Jesus in the Blessed Sacrament will make all our crosses sweet and easy to carry, and by them He will make us saints as He did His Holy Mother.

The sufferings of the flight soon came to an end, like all things temporal, and the Holy Family enjoyed after the exile the long years of peace in the quiet home at Nazareth.

> How shalt thou bear the Cross that now
>   So dread a weight appears?
> Keep quietly to God and think
>   Upon the eternal years.

Janssens

THE THIRD SORROW—THE THREE DAYS' LOSS

CHAPTER VIII

The Three Days' Loss

DURING the long and we may say happy years of the hidden life of Jesus at Nazareth, only one great sorrow is recorded by the Evangelist. It was a sorrow of short duration, but it certainly was the keenest yet felt by Mary. The three days' loss would have been sufficient to fulfill the prophecy of holy Simeon because the heart of Mary was certainly pierced by the sword of anguish, and we may almost say of despair. During the sorrows of the first Christmas night, Mary has her Jesus with her for the Redemption of mankind. In the Presentation in the Temple, when holy Simeon foretold her future sorrows, she carried Jesus in her arms, and she could bear with any cross, so long as she possessed Jesus. In the flight into Egypt, Mary felt all the anguish of exile and all the inconveniences of the long journey, but still she had her Son, and so deep down in her soul she enjoyed peace in the midst of her distress and suffering.

But in the loss of Jesus for three days, matters were quite different, and even her one consolation, Jesus, was taken from her. Oh, the anguish of Mary and her interior desolation at the loss of Jesus! She had received from God the great mission to preserve Jesus and bring Him up to manhood for the great work of founding the Church for the Redemption of the world. She had performed her task well in the midst of contradictions and persecutions, and by her patience in suffering she had acquired great graces so that her personality became more beautiful and more attractive as the years wore on. Her sorrows during the Holy Infancy had brought about a seriousness of character and a sweetness of disposition which could mark her off to the intelligent eye as someone destined for something great. Her kindness and sweetness were supernaturalized by past sorrows, which had made her more recollected than ever, and the heavenly beauty of her soul was shown by her serene though serious countenance.

When the Boy Jesus was twelve years old, He was brought to Jerusalem for the feast of the Pasch. Great crowds gathered from all parts of the country and from the surrounding Jewish colonies to celebrate this feast. On the return journey Jesus leaves His parents quietly, and He was not missed until Mary and Joseph camped for the night in one of the towns on the homeward journey. They then for the first time learn that Jesus is not with them, and they return in great anguish of mind in search of Him. It is very difficult even to attempt to describe the unutterable desolation of Mary during the search for Jesus.

Up to that time she had at least managed to preserve the life of Jesus, but now He was lost, and she did not know what had become of Him. Had she after all her sufferings during the Holy Infancy been unfaithful to her charge, and had she failed in her great mission? These thoughts passed through the mind of Mary, and she did not know what answer to give to them. Had she failed in the trust confided to her keeping by God Himself through the ministry of an archangel? She always had Jesus by her side during the twelve years of His life, but now He was gone and perhaps the fault was hers. Mary had a tender heart, and by the sorrows of the Holy Infancy she had been gaining a greater insight into the manner of the accomplishment of the Redemption, and she realized the greatness of her responsibility; but this only increased her anguish and desolation of soul. We may have sometimes witnessed a mother in sorrow at the death of her child, or we may have sympathized with an aged parent in her grief at the departure of an only child from the home of its mother, but in these cases the grief-stricken parent has at least the consolation of knowing that the child has passed out of this world or has gone to another home; but Mary had not only to suffer the anguish of loss, but also the more terrible sufferings of doubt and uncertainty. Where was Jesus? She did not know and yet she was responsible for Him. If He were lost, the fault might, she thought, be rightly attributed to her. Oh, the desolation of the sweet heart of Mary at the uncertainty of the whole thing! Jesus had never left her before, and what was the cause of this separation from her. Mary received no heavenly consolation during the three days, and when at last she finds Jesus, she gives expression to her feelings of grief in words which indicate her maternal care for Jesus. She says, "Son, why hast thou done so to us? Behold thy father and I have sought thee sorrowing."

In the answer to His Holy Mother, Jesus utters very precious words. They are the first words recorded of Jesus during His life up to that time. "Did you not know," He says, "that I must be about My Father's business?" Jesus during the three days' loss leaves His Holy Mother, although He knew it would cause her terrible suffering and desolation. His Holy Mother had been sanctified by the making of many sacrifices during the Holy Infancy. She had clung to the happiness of the sensible presence of Jesus, and Her Divine Son now wished to sanctify her still more by detaching her even from this consolation. Jesus withdrew from her for a time to prepare her for a greater and more complete sacrifice later and to teach her also that His life work was not always to be amidst the domestic duties of Nazareth. We see how the sorrows of Mary become deeper and how each one is a preparation for a greater sorrow and a more heroic renunciation later. From this sorrow and from the words of Jesus, Mary realized more than ever the importance of the work of Redemption, and she was prepared for the great separation after the Hidden Life had come to an end.

Mary lost the sensible presence of Jesus and suffered terrible anguish of soul for another reason also. All spiritual writers call Mary the "Refuge of Sinners," and we see wonderful conversions after lifelong sins once the sinner has recourse to Mary and once he asks her to intercede for him. By the anguish of the three days' loss she has gained the right to intercede on behalf of those who lose Jesus by sin.

After the depth of the desolation of the three days' loss, the heart of Mary becomes more tender still. Each sorrow enlarges her sympathies for the poor and the afflicted, and who are poorer than those who have lost Jesus by sin. Some cannot understand the power of the intercession of Mary on behalf of sinners and of the afflicted, but these do not understand all the depth and desolation of the three days' loss. How her maternal heart pleads for sinners, and what efforts she makes for their salvation! Jesus wished His Holy Mother to be the consoler of the afflicted and the helper of the sinner, and so He prepared her heart for this great work by permitting her to suffer the three days' loss and to enable her to gain grace so that she could afterwards save souls by her powerful intercession.

This third dolor of Our Lady has been a very fortunate occurrence for us, and through the great grief of the three days' loss many souls have reached everlasting happiness through Mary's prayers. She then for the first time realized what Jesus meant to her and to the world, and she has now compassion on the suffering and sorrowful and on all those who are deprived of Jesus through mortal sin. By her prayers she has been instrumental in saving many millions of souls from Hell, and she would never allow a soul to enter this place of torment if her intercession could keep the soul from it. If the greatest sinners would only accept the assistance of Mary, they would soon be restored to God's friendship. Oh, how she pleads with her Divine Son on behalf of sinners, but too often her pleadings are in vain, simply because the sinner will not accept the graces which Mary asks and obtains for him. When we pray to Our Lady to assist us in times of temptation, we thereby express our willingness to accept her gifts and her protection. Those who do not pray to Mary show that they have no desire to receive her gifts, and therefore Our Dear Lady cannot help them, simply because they refuse her aid. Our Blessed Mother and her Divine Son are engaged trying to keep people from walking into Hell.

Oh, how the Sacred Heart of Jesus and the Immaculate Heart of Mary yearn for the salvation of a soul! What anguish do these pure hearts not suffer during the years spent in this world for the sake of sinners and to think that so many are lost simply because they will not accept the gifts she has at hand for them. When will it be realized the wonderful power of Mary for the conversion of sinners, and when will those who are in fear of being lost for eternity learn to have recourse to this tender-hearted Mother! We have merely to ask her to assist us. She has graces to dispense to all those who will accept them. Who has ever heard of a soul having recourse to Mary and yet being finally lost? Who has ever yet approached Mary in earnestness and asked for her assistance and has ever yet been refused? Those who wish to do much for Jesus ought first of all to ask this sweet Mother to protect them from all the powers of earth and Hell. The devils are powerless once Mary is approached. Oh, when will people ever learn that they have in Mary a Mother and a protector who can overcome all the powers of Hell and who can protect the Church in all dangers! Devotion to Mary is the mark of sanctity and the best guarantee of reaching a great crown of glory for eternity. It is a beautiful devotion to recite the Beads of the Seven Dolors [see Appendix] for the conversion of sinners. She wishes us to assist her in saving souls. If the faithful only once realized the great treasures and the sweet communications Mary gives to her children, all the world would seek her for a Mother and protector.

> O Mary, my Mother, so tender so true,
>   In all my afflictions I hasten to you:
> Your heart is so gentle, so loving, so mild,
>   You cannot reject your poor suppliant child.
>
> O Mary, my Mother, so meek and so mild,
>   Look down upon me, a poor sinful child;
> Secure me, 'midst dangers, from enemies free,
>   And conduct me at death unto Jesus and thee.

THE FINDING OF THE CHILD JESUS IN THE TEMPLE

THE HIDDEN LIFE

CHAPTER IX

Mary during the Hidden Life

IT IS unfortunate that so little attention is paid to the hidden life of Jesus and Mary during the thirty years spent at Nazareth before Our Lord began His Public Life. Jesus during these years obeyed His parents, and this obedience of Jesus extended to all the details of domestic life and was given with a promptness and an inward joy simply because He wished to teach a great lesson for all future ages and to give an example of submission to lawful authority for a higher end. Jesus obeyed because it was His Father's will that He should be subjected to His parents, and in the obedience to their commands He gained graces for all those who have to live in subjection, that they might sanctify their obedience by doing everything and obeying their lawful superiors, simply to please God and to sanctify themselves.

But what are we to say of Mary during the hidden life of Jesus? Oh, what a subject worthy of meditation: Jesus obeying His Mother and St. Joseph during thirty years and not giving, even to them, any proof of His divinity! He toiled at the carpenter's bench and assisted His Holy Mother in the duties of the household, and yet as far as we can learn, He never manifested even once His power or His wisdom because it was not the will of His Father. These thirty years were a great test of the faith and trust of Mary and St. Joseph. Very many falsely think that Jesus made known to His Holy Mother many divine secrets and told her of future events so that she might be consoled by the knowledge of His future glory and of the future greatness of the Church. All this again is only the product of a sentimental mind, which is unable to grasp the deep mystery of faith and confidence. We may safely say that Jesus told Mary nothing of His future glory, nor did she receive any supernatural manifestations of His power and knowledge. The archangel Gabriel appeared once to Mary and told her that she was to be the Mother of the Saviour and that Jesus would save the people from their sins, and this was the only supernatural manifestation of His dignity she received during her lifetime.

In fact, it would be strange if it were otherwise when we now contemplate her glory. During the flight into Egypt, Mary carried Jesus in her arms, and yet she received no manifestation of His power. She had to flee even to preserve His life. At the three days' loss she is overwhelmed with grief, but Jesus gives her no comfort. During those thirty years, Jesus gave her no information concerning His mission, nor did she ask for any. At the marriage feast of Cana she merely said to her Son, "They have no wine." This amounted to a command to work a miracle, and she knew He would not refuse nor even give the least pretext of disobedience to her, but yet He treated her without any mark of personal or sentimental affection. These years at Nazareth were profitable years for Mary because each day she was growing in grace and gaining by the least good action an additional degree of merit. Each little action was performed solely for the love of Jesus, and she had no thought of herself in all her sufferings and sacrifices. She asked no questions about the future nor about the secrets of Heaven because this would have rendered her good actions less meritorious. Her faith was tested far beyond that of the Apostles.

The Apostles saw Our Lord's miracles and they were instructed in the truths of the Gospel by Jesus Himself, but when the time of trial came during His Passion, they were scandalized and they fled. Mary saw very few miracles, nor did she wish to see them. Her faith and trust had no need of miracles. She asked Jesus no questions about His mission because that was His own secret, and the revelation of His dignity was only to be made known according to the time and manner which was pleasing to His Father and according to the preparations made by the people for the reception of the good tidings. Mary asked for no miracles during the hidden life, although she might have been excused for asking for a miracle at least during the flight into Egypt. During the exile, the Holy Family bore with the inconveniences of the strange country in a spirit of interior joy and so sanctified themselves by their cheerful conformity with God's will. They did not indulge in sentimental longings for their native country, nor did they give way to the feelings of homesickness because, by doing so, they would have taken back some of the sacrifices they so willingly performed during the exile.

It is time now to give a reason for the apparent indifference of Jesus towards His Mother and His want of sentimental affection for her. Why again did not Mary insist upon her maternal rights and make use of her position of Mother to gain advantages from Jesus and secure freedom from cares and trials, as so many in the world would certainly have endeavored to do. Jesus had good reason for not showing His sweet Mother any sentimental affection. He wished to sanctify her more and more, and He was most anxious that His Mother should not lose one degree of glory for eternity.

His apparent indifference to her wants and His refraining from showing any sentiments of love towards her were really proofs of His tender love for her. Had He given her consolations and sweetness and had He bestowed upon her all the endearments prompted by nature, He would have been depriving her of very much merit, and He would have made her less sympathetic with the suffering and the sorrowful. Mary received no heavenly consolations, and she had no manifestations of the power of her Divine Son: He was born in poverty; He had to flee from Herod; and He worked like an ordinary laborer. Jesus gave no proof of His divinity during the thirty years and never even told Mary of His eternal existence before coming to this world. Here was a great test of Mary's faith and confidence. The angel had assured her and she wished for no more proofs, nor did she receive any during the thirty years of the Hidden Life.

It might be remarked that Jesus would surely make known many heavenly secrets to His Holy Mother in order to console her for all her sacrifices. This again is confusing the meaning of sanctification. Jesus wished His sweet Mother to receive the full reward for her faith as well as for her other sacrifices. Some holy souls are troubled because they receive no sensible proofs of God's love and because Our Lord gives them no encouragement in all their works and sufferings. In carrying on a good work for Our Lord's glory, it often seems that God has deserted His chosen friends and thus leaves them to themselves. This is only a device of the beautiful Heart of Jesus to give His friends the opportunity of gaining the full merit of their trust and confidence. Mary trusted in Jesus amidst all the humiliations of Good Friday, and even on the cross Jesus addresses her without any marks of affection.

It is quite probable that He never once appeared to her after His Resurrection, nor did she receive any sensible consolation even after Our Lord's Ascension. The remembrance of Good Friday was for her a source of perpetual sorrow, and she longed more and more for final union with Jesus, but yet she never asked Jesus to hasten the hour of her death. The dolors of Mary did not end with the laying of the body of Jesus in the Sepulcher. The tortures of the Crucifixion had so affected her that she bore ever afterwards the impress of a crushing sorrow, and her final years may have been years of interior desolation on account of the remembrance of Good Friday. Jesus deprived Mary of all sensible consolation and asked her to bear a lifelong cross in order to raise her up to unspeakable heights of glory. Every moment of sensible consolation, every word of sentimental affection, and every manifestation of God's friendship would have taken something from the glory of Mary, and Jesus loved her too well to deprive her of the least degree of happiness for eternity.

We may derive great profit from reflection on the thirty years of the hidden life of Mary, during which time she always carried the lifelong cross of the prophecy of holy Simeon. It is such a pity that so many earnest souls do not sanctify themselves more by their resignation to God's will in the performance of their everyday duties. Mary grew in grace every day of her life simply because she did everything for the sake of Jesus. She united her sufferings and prayers with those of Jesus for the salvation of souls.

Some again are anxious for revelations and expect that God will show them some external or sensible proof of His love. Jesus may in the beginning give to His friends and spouses some sign of His love and make known His Holy will in some sweet way, but after having done so, He allows them to go on in darkness in order to give them the reward of trust and confidence. Every manifestation made then would only deprive the soul of grace, and Jesus loves us so much that He is anxious to have us near Him for eternity, and so He gives us opportunities of acquiring merit. Jesus dislikes one sin or one fault above all others, and that is want of confidence. His sweet Mother never wounded His Sacred Heart in this way. She trusted Jesus during the silence of the hidden life. She trusted Him amidst the desolation of Calvary. She trusted Him even when He appeared to others after His Resurrection and never once came to her. Mary had not to trust long.

Her short and useful life came to an end, and then her reward commenced. She can now obtain everything from Jesus, and she is well rewarded for her confidence. Oh, if we would, like Mary, trust in Jesus, in spite of all desolation and amidst all the sorrows of this life, we would also, like Mary, sanctify ourselves and gain the immortal crown of glory. Some are anxious for their salvation and fear they may not be in God's friendship. Oh if they would, like Mary, leave all their cares upon Jesus, they would be raised up in the last day. This confidence in Jesus will raise us up to a position in Heaven which will reward us for our trust amidst the desolation of all the crosses and trials of this life. Mary forgot herself all during life and thought only of Jesus. Let us imitate her and cease our indulging in sentimental complaints or in searching for sensible consolation. We ought to help Jesus in the salvation of souls by offering our works and sufferings for the conversion of sinners and by praying for the spread of the Faith. We can rest for eternity.

> Thy self-upbraiding is a snare,
>   Though meekness it appears;
> More humbling it is far for thee
>   To face the eternal years.

Bottoni

THE HOLY FAMILY

Bida

CHRIST TEACHING IN THE SYNAGOGUE

CHAPTER X

The Departure of Jesus from Nazareth

THE Public Life of Jesus began when He was thirty years old. He remained in subjection and in seclusion much longer than most boys, but the happy period of the hidden life had to come to an end because Jesus had yet to fulfill His great mission of founding His Church and of dying for the Redemption of mankind. The departure of Jesus from Nazareth, where He had spent the long and peaceful years in company with the holiest and most lovable of creatures, caused great interior sorrow to Jesus, but when the time came, He was equal to the occasion and went forth to do the will of His Heavenly Father.

The departure of Jesus was another great sorrow to Mary. So great was the trial for Mary at the departure of Jesus that she had been prepared for it eighteen years previously by the sorrow of the three days' loss. Jesus then said to her, "Did you not know that I must be about my Father's business," and this was really a preparation for the long and more painful separation of His Public Life. Mary too was ready for the sacrifice of giving up Jesus. She had enjoyed His presence for half her lifetime, but now He was to leave her, and the separation was to be complete and was to end only when Mary would join Him in the never-ending peace of Paradise. During the Public Life, Mary saw little of Jesus, and on the few occasions when they met as if by accident, Jesus gave her no manifestations of His love. On the Cross He handed her over to the care of St. John, and so we may conclude that the departure of Jesus from His home at Nazareth was a source of silent grief to both Jesus and Mary.

The manner in which Mary bore the grief of the

departure of Jesus has given courage to and obtained grace for parents to part with their children when God calls them to a higher vocation. Jesus could often have visited His Mother during His Public Life, but we never once hear that He did so. Whenever He met His Holy Mother during the Public Life, He never indulged in sentimental marks of affection, nor did He in the least lessen her great sacrifice.

Both Jesus and Mary had made the great sacrifice of being separated from each other, and neither of them took any part of the sacrifice back again. Jesus here had to teach a great lesson and give an example which would last for all time. Parents are often asked by God to make a sacrifice of their children for Our Lord's sake, and some will make the sacrifice only half-heartedly. They still wish to have their children near them, and they still hope to have the pleasure of their company at least occasionally.

Children often refuse the call of Jesus for fear of the sacrifice it might cost their dear ones. This is false love on the part of both parents and children. Jesus loved Mary as no son ever loved a mother, and yet He left her, although St. Joseph had died and she was alone. Why did Jesus treat His Holy Mother with such apparent indifference to her maternal feelings? Had He no filial affection for her? Yes, Jesus and Mary loved each other and enjoyed each other's company, but Jesus wished His Holy Mother to receive the full merit of the sacrifice of the separation. Mary bore with her loneliness during the Public Life of Jesus and never once wished to have Him with her again during life because she had made the sacrifice of His company and she would not take back any of the offering she made at the departure of Jesus. During the three years of the Public Life, Mary may often have endured the pangs of loneliness and may have felt deep sorrow and abandonment at the loss of Jesus and on account of the opposition to His works from the jealousy of the Pharisees, but she never once asked Him to return to her, nor does she ever visit Him. Mary grew in grace and in merit each day by her renewal of the sacrifice of the separation. We have no reason to wonder at the marvels of the powers of Mary now that she is in Heaven, nor need we be surprised at the glories she has received from the Church. She refused Jesus no sacrifice while she was on this earth, and now Jesus can refuse her nothing. We see here the deep and supernatural love of Jesus for His Holy Mother.

He wished her to lose no merit, and so He gives her the opportunity of gaining additional grace every moment of her life. The separation during the Public Life might have been softened by interior consolation or by the promise of their future reunion. But Jesus did not wish to soften the desolation of the departure from His Holy Mother. During the three years of the Public Life, Jesus gave no consolation to Mary, and He seemed to be quite indifferent to her. This was again to increase her merit. Mary bore during those years the agony of the prophecy of holy Simeon. She knew that a terrible sorrow was in store for her and she knew that Jesus would be a sign of contradiction. This was a perpetual sorrow in her heart and she carried this to her dying day. This sorrow was now increased and part of the prophecy fulfilled by the separation from Jesus. This increased sorrow of Mary was borne each day without consolation from Jesus. Jesus certainly could have softened the sorrows of Mary by His visits and by His words of consolation, but these acts of sentimental affection never took place. Jesus loved her too much to deprive her of the least degree of grace, and if He had appeared to her to soften her affliction, both would have taken back some of the sacrifices they so generously made. Mary gained grace every moment of her life by her resignation under her lifelong and daily-increasing sorrows. She offered each suffering in union with those of Jesus for the salvation of souls. In this way she gained grace after grace, and so we can now realize the reason for her glory in Heaven.

The lifelong sorrows of Mary teach us a far-reaching lesson. Very many have sorrows to bear, but they lose much of the merit of their crosses because they will not bear them in union with Jesus and for the sake of Jesus. Mary joined her sufferings with the sufferings of Jesus for the salvation of souls, and if we would only imitate Mary in this patient carrying of our daily crosses, we would very soon sanctify ourselves and gain great merit for eternity. Again, too many take back a part of the sacrifices they once made. This is a great cause of mediocrity or of the absence of great zeal for Our Lord's interests. They wish to receive some marks of love and affection from those who are dear to them, or they wish to enjoy the pleasure of their company at least occasionally. This is merely taking back part of the sacrifices. Some again seek for sensible consolations from Jesus, and they foolishly think that Jesus is not pleased with them when He does not load them with the temporal blessings and spiritual consolations. Jesus loved Mary more than anybody ever loved a mother, and yet He gave her no exterior proofs of His affection nor did He soften the bitterness of her desolation. In fact Mary only wished for what Jesus wished, and so she asked for no consolation. She wished to make the full sacrifice and to give everything to Jesus. How many souls are so deceived by the devil and by the allurements of the world that they lose confidence in Jesus as soon as He sends them a little cross or takes from them His sensible consolations.

In the departure of Jesus from Nazareth we can also appreciate the strong and lovable personality of Mary. It is such a pity that the beautiful and resourceful personality of Mary is not made a subject of more frequent consideration. Her mission was to cooperate with her Divine Son in the salvation of the world, and she well carried out her task. We see her strength of character on the first Christmas night—when she could find no place wherein to rest herself, how she made the best of the manger and the straw and the swaddling bands. When Herod wished to kill Jesus, she promptly obeyed the command to fly into Egypt. During the three days' loss, she sought for Jesus until she found Him. In this case, Mary was overwhelmed with grief at the loss of Jesus, and she was saddened still more to think that perhaps the fault was hers that Jesus was lost.

In this case she does not give way to sentimental melancholy, nor does she waste her time in useless regrets, which are often only manifestations of disappointed vanity. She at once sets off to find Jesus and never ceases her search until she has cast her loving eyes upon Him. At the departure from Nazareth, Mary does not ask Jesus to prolong His stay with her for one day longer than was pleasing to Him because she would not consider her own feelings when it was a question of the salvation of souls. Oh, what a strong and lovable personality was that of Mary. At the marriage feast the wine ran short, but Mary was there and her intelligent and resourceful mind found a way of procuring wine—and without even directly asking for a miracle. She merely says to Jesus, "They have no wine." During the Public Life, while the people were applauding her Divine Son, she never appeared. She was too deep of character and possessed the gifts of the Holy Ghost so much that she could not be taken in by the emptiness of popular applause. She never forgot that all the applause would one day be changed into shouts of mockery and derision. Oh, how many lose grace and sell their souls for the empty and passing applause of the crowd or else act to please men instead of thinking only of pleasing God. Mary realized that Jesus was everything in time and eternity and all other passing and vain things were not worthy of a moment's consideration. She was so supernatural and her intellect was so deep and so clear that she easily realized the worthlessness of the friendship of the so-called great people, and hence she remained in retirement during those years because her vocation was not to be before the public eye. It mattered not to Mary so long as Jesus was able to carry out His divine mission. We see here the wisdom of Jesus in choosing for His Mother one so intelligent and of such a strong and sweet personality. Jesus owed very much of the sweetness and strength of His own character and dispositions to Mary. He was truly Her Son, and it was she who was responsible for His early education.

We can learn from this self-sacrifice of Mary in parting with Jesus the great lesson of generosity in God's service. We ought to serve God without looking for any earthly consolation and without thinking about the reward. Jesus wishes for a disinterested love which alone is true love. He says, ''My child, give Me thy heart.'' Mary gave everything to Jesus and asked for nothing in return. She is now enjoying the reward of her generosity to Jesus while on this earth. How well she earned all her glory. How Jesus now enjoys the presence of His Holy Mother in Heaven.

Plockhorst

JESUS BLESSING THE CHILDREN

Janssens

FOURTH SORROW—MEETING JESUS CARRYING HIS CROSS

CHAPTER XI

The Meeting with Jesus Carrying His Cross

THE MEETING with Jesus, carrying His Cross up the hill of Calvary, is called Our Lady's fourth dolor. It would be more correct to say that this grief of Mary embraced the scourging and the crowning with thorns and lasted during the journey up the long hill to the place of Crucifixion. It is not known with certainty what time Mary joined the crowd who were following Jesus. She was very likely present at the cruel scourging because this was the greatest of all the bodily sufferings of Jesus, and in order to increase her merit and to gain her prayers for souls, it is very likely that Jesus wished His Mother to be present during the flagellation and the mockery of the Crowning with Thorns. Pilate in his cowardice condemns Jesus to death, and to increase the shame and ignominy of the Crucifixion, Jesus is made to carry His own heavy Cross up to the summit of Calvary.

The scourging had so exhausted the strength of Jesus that His whole frame was ruined. The scourging was really the killing of Jesus, but still the cruelty of the executioners makes them place the heavy weight of the Cross upon His bleeding shoulders. Jesus had not gone far with the Cross when His strength gave way and He fell exhausted to the ground under its heavy weight. While He is struggling to lift the Cross, His Holy Mother comes up to Him and their eyes meet. Jesus had not seen His Mother for some time, nor did Mary know what kind of death was in store for Her Divine Son. She knew from the prophecy of holy Simeon that her heart would one day be pierced with sorrow, but she never could even conceive during her lifetime of such cruelty and ignominy as that in which she now beheld Jesus. It was well for Mary that she had gained grace and had been prepared by her early dolors for this terrible scene of Jesus going up the hill of Calvary on the first Good Friday. Jesus was bent almost to the ground under the weight of the heavy Cross. He is staggering at every step and can only move along very slowly on account of His weakness. The blood has been flowing from His body during the greater part of the morning, and it is now ebbing away drop by drop, and soon it will be exhausted.

The crowd surges around on all sides, and among all those heedless people not one takes His part nor offers a word of sympathy. Those who were the friends of Jesus during His life now join with the rabble in their shouts of mockery and derision. Only one in all that crowd could appreciate fully the immensity of the sufferings of Jesus. The holy women wept for Him, but their tears were more of pity than of sincere sympathy. Veronica gave Jesus a towel, and some other holy women followed Jesus and remained faithful to the end, but none of them had the deep grace or the enlightened mind of Mary to understand all the agonies of soul and body through which Jesus was passing. What mother was ever yet asked to witness such sufferings at the deathbed of a dying child as Mary was asked to endure on the first Good Friday? Mary wishes to give Jesus just one word of comfort and sympathy in His sufferings. The Apostles have fled, and no one is there to comfort or offer even a word of sympathy to Jesus or to assure Him that He is not altogether without friends. Mary wishes to tell Jesus that there was at least one loving heart, but she is rudely pushed aside, and instead of sympathy Jesus receives only blows and kicks. Instead of kind words, Jesus hears only the shouts of mockery and insult.

The crowd moves on up the hill, but it soon becomes apparent to the Jews that Jesus cannot carry the Cross. His strength is exhausted on account of the cruelty and brutality of the Scourging, but not one in the crowd offers to assist Jesus with the Cross. Mary is in the midst of the crowd and she hears all the blasphemies and mockeries which are uttered against her Divine Son. The other holy women pitied Jesus, but Mary realized the injustice of the condemnation and of the Crucifixion. She had learned to love Jesus as no mother ever loved a son, not only because He was her Child, but also because she realized His goodness and greatness of soul and the kindness and sweetness of His character.

It is almost impossible to fathom the depth and tenderness of a mother's love. The mother's heart feels keenly the sufferings of her child. Oh, what desolation, what abyss of grief was in the heart of Mary as she followed her Divine Son up the hill of Calvary. She often came near Him, and she saw the cruel blows and kicks that were being heaped upon Him. While looking at the sweet face of Jesus—that countenance she had so often in His infancy pressed to her heart—she beheld the expression of unspeakable anguish and suffering. Their eyes meet each other. They do not speak because the crowd is urging on their Victim and the people are thirsting for blood. Mary would have wished to embrace Jesus, but she is not allowed even this consolation. Mary cast her sweet maternal eyes on Jesus, but this only increased the sufferings of both. Jesus fixed His gaze for a moment on His Holy Mother, but oh, this gaze of inexpressible anguish, sorrow, and pain was really the fulfillment of Simeon's prophecy!

This look of unutterable anguish pierced the loving heart of Mary as no other sorrow had ever yet done. Mary experienced terrible grief during the three days' loss, but then she thought her Jesus might be lost and her work unaccomplished. She did not mind so much the sorrow she endured if only she could find Jesus. Now she sees her dear Son suffering tortures so great that even she could never have dreamt of. This look of Jesus revealed to Mary another source of sorrow which sent the sword of Simeon deeper and deeper into the most secret recesses of her heart and broke the most tender cords of maternal affection. The bodily anguish of the Scourging, the heavy weight of the Cross and the insults of the crowd were like deluges of sorrow to crush the sweet heart of Mary. But the glance of Jesus revealed to her a much deeper and more oppressive sorrow.

The expression of anguish on the countenance of Jesus revealed to the Mother's Heart that Jesus was suffering all these bodily tortures while His soul was steeped in the depth of desolation and abandonment. Mary herself was enduring all the interior anguish of spiritual desolation. Oh, her soul is plunged into a sea of grief! The sorrows and interior desolation of Mary were so extensive that they embraced every faculty of her soul and sought out even the deepest recesses of maternal tenderness. In most cases of suffering there are generally some rays of hope and some star of consolation to be found in the deepest night of sorrow, but no hope and no consolation is left for Mary. Every avenue of happiness is closed up, and she remains immersed in an ocean of sorrow and desolation. Yet she never deserts Jesus nor does she pray to be released from even one anguish of her maternal heart. The sufferings of Jesus pierced the heart of Mary with swords of anguish and desolation, but she never asks for the sufferings of Jesus to be lessened because she would never take back any part of the sacrifice made in accepting the great task of being the Mother of Jesus.

During the journey to Calvary, in the midst of desolation so great that it surpasses all the sufferings of the martyrs, and when her soul is steeped in the terrible trials of interior abandonment, Mary never once uttered so much as one cry of impatience, nor did she even ask to receive the least ray of consolation. She felt no resentment towards the soldiers nor towards the people who were thus ill-treating her Son. She had compassion on their willful blindness, and she prayed for their salvation with all the tenderness of her maternal heart. How she prayed for the two thieves who were crucified with Jesus; and when she hears one of the thieves expressing sentiments of sorrow and love, oh how her sweet heart rejoices in the midst of her desolation at the salvation of this poor soul.

She prays for those around the Cross, and when she hears the Roman official expressing words of faith in Jesus, she rejoices more than ever because she realized that the sufferings of Jesus have not been in vain and that they will reach even to the Gentiles and eventually to all the peoples of the world. Mary was not content to pray only for those around the Cross. She prayed with all the enthusiasm of a soul which had been enlightened on the value of the Redemption and on the importance of the salvation of souls and for the success of the Church during future ages. How her heart offered fervent prayers to God that the sufferings of Jesus might at least not be in vain. She prayed for Judas, but Judas would not accept the graces offered. She felt keenly the loss of Judas. He had once been a friend of Jesus, and she loved dearly all whom Jesus loved, and Jesus loved Judas and tried hard to save the fallen Apostle by addressing him by the sweet name of friend. Both Jesus and Mary felt keenly the loss of Judas, but Judas would not accept all the promptings of grace which were seeking admittance into the soul of that wretched Apostle. Mary realized then as she had never realized before the value of an immortal soul, and she made good use of her time in praying for the conversion of all sinners and for the spread of the blessings of Jesus throughout the world. It will never be known on this side of eternity how many millions of souls owe their salvation to the prayers of Mary on the first Good Friday. She prayed for the Apostles and for Peter in particular, and her prayers were all heard because they were uttered by a soul filled with God's grace and while she was suffering tortures of interior anguish.

We may learn from this great dolor of Mary the importance of sanctifying our sufferings by uniting them with those of Jesus and by bearing them with patience. We could gain much grace and save many souls if we would, like Our Lady, offer our sufferings for the conversion of sinners. Prayer during suffering will be all powerful and it will also obtain grace to sanctify ourselves. It will be astonishing when we shall realize how many souls owe their salvation to Mary's prayers on the first Good Friday. We have also an opportunity of praying with great efficacy during the Holy Sacrifice of the Mass. The Mass is the renewal of the sufferings of Calvary, and at the moment of Consecration, if we would stand in spirit at the foot of the Cross with Our Lady and there pray for the conversion of sinners, the needs of the Church, as well as for our own needs, our prayers would be efficacious, and we would go away from Mass filled with graces and blessings. To hear Mass with devotion and to be present at all the Masses possible is very pleasing to the Sacred Hearts of Jesus and Mary.

THE SORROWFUL MOTHER MEETS JESUS

Janssens

FIFTH SORROW—THE DEATH OF JESUS

CHAPTER XII

Mary Stands beneath the Cross of Jesus

WHO will ever be able to describe or even conceive a fraction of the sufferings of Mary during the three hours while Jesus was hanging on the Cross on the first Good Friday. The darkness and the earthquake had caused many to move away from the Cross, but Mary stood there to the end in the midst of a sea of sorrows. Very many think of Mary's sorrows as they think of the sorrows of a mother watching by the bedside of a dying child. These sorrows endured by mothers at the loss or at the sufferings of their children are certainly faint resemblances of the sorrows of Mary while she stands beneath the Cross, but we might combine all the sorrows of all the mothers in the world, and yet they would not when added together equal the sufferings of Mary. During her whole lifetime Mary had been growing in grace. She bore within her soul the sword of the prophecy of holy Simeon, which caused her desolation of soul all the days of her life. She had gained much grace by the sufferings of the three days' loss, and every day during the thirty years at Nazareth, she grew in grace as she grew in age. What was the reason for this long period of preparation between the three days' loss and the greater sorrow of Calvary? These years were required so to sanctify the soul of Mary and so to fill her with all graces and all sweetness of disposition as to enable her to bear the anguish of the Crucifixion. Mary had to bear all the sorrows of Calvary in the midst of interior darkness and desolation of soul. The faith and trust of Mary were put to the test on that day, and she stood the test well.

The friends of Jesus lost faith in Him when they saw Him in such humiliation. Could this really be the Son of God when He was so weak and helpless in the presence of His enemies? Was it true, after all, that He was not really the Messias? Again, others lost confidence in Jesus in the midst of His sufferings. What good would Jesus do them when He was not able to save Himself? Was He really worth following if He could only offer to His followers the ignominy of the Cross? Yes, very few even of the most cherished of the friends of Jesus were able to stand the test of all the disgrace of Good Friday. We see this in the history of the Church. In times of persecution the weak have not sufficient faith and hope to follow Jesus in the midst of suffering.

When any good work is started in the Church for the salvation of souls, we will always find that it must be built on the Cross, as the Church itself was built on the humiliations of the first Good Friday. When a saint is raised up by God to do great work for souls, it will always be found that the work is built on the Cross, and very many will give a helping hand so long as matters prosper, but they quickly fall away in the face of obstacles or ridicule. They join the crowd just as the hollow friends of Jesus joined the rabble on the first Good Friday. They are scandalized at the weakness of those who are chosen by God to carry out great works, falsely thinking that souls are saved by worldly wisdom or by worldly power. Mary was practically the only single soul that never lost the least confidence in Jesus nor ever for a moment wavered in her faith. This was a tremendous test of greatness of soul.

Some may think that Jesus foretold to His Mother all the events of His Passion and all the future glory of His Resurrection, but there is really no reason for thinking so, and Mary may never have even known the nature of the sufferings of Jesus before the first Good Friday. She asked for no proof of the divinity of Jesus. Her faith was too deep to need proof. She never lost confidence in Jesus in the midst of all the interior desolation with which she was engulfed. Those who have experienced the anguish of abandonment can realize that no other suffering can equal this abyss of loneliness and desolation. Some of the saints have suffered for years this interior trial when God seems to have deserted the soul, and there seems to be nothing left but an abyss of indescribable loneliness and when the soul seems to be utterly deserted by God. The saints persevered in their trust in God in the midst of this interior anguish, and as a reward for their trust Jesus gave them great glory for eternity.

But the desolation of Mary might be compared to a soul sinking down into unfathomable regions of nothingness where the soul is so isolated that the interior anguish of mind is sufficient to drive one to despair. This was still just the substratum of the griefs of Mary on the first Good Friday. The agonies of Jesus so pierced her soul and cut through her tender heart that it was almost a miracle that Mary did not die of grief with her Divine Son when she received His dead body in her arms. After Jesus had arrived at the summit of Calvary, He is stripped of His garments. The rude soldiers then throw Jesus on the Cross and while one kneels on His chest, another drives the nails through His hands and feet. Mary hears the blows of the hammer as the nails pierce through those tender hands which had so often worked for her at Nazareth. Those feet, which had been used in going after souls and had often been sore from the weary journeys of the long days' work in their mission for the welfare of others, were now nailed to their bed of torture. Mary sees the tender body of Jesus, which she had nursed in its infancy and watched in its development and growth during the years of boyhood, now exposed to the jeers and mockery of the thoughtless and empty-headed rabble. Oh, how her maternal eyes rested on the body of her Jesus as He lies attached to His bed of pain. The Cross is raised on high, and it drops into the place prepared for it. Every jerk sends unspeakable anguish through the maternal heart of Mary. And now Jesus is hanging on the Cross. She looks into His face, but the anguish and the expression of pain on the sweet countenance of Jesus pierces her heart through and through. Will the sufferings of Jesus never come to an end? In all those thirty odd years since the prophecy of Simeon, Mary may have gone over in her mind and prepared herself for the great sufferings necessary for the Redemption, but she could never think of anything so great as those she witnessed on Calvary.

During the three hours which seemed to the sweet heart of Mary to be never ending, Jesus cries out, "I thirst." What would not Mary have given to have been able to relieve the thirst of Jesus. She looked up again into the beautiful countenance of Jesus, with the terrible expression of deep desolation and pain painted on those heavenly features. She sees the lips parched and cracked. She sees the blood dropping very slowly, and the last drops are falling down to the ground. She realizes the terrible fire that is consuming Jesus, but she cannot even give Him a single drop of water. She cannot even approach near enough to offer her sympathy or to express her maternal feelings. Oh, who will ever describe the piercing anguish of the heart of Mary when she heard Jesus uttering the cry of thirst from the inmost recesses of His tortured heart! But Mary had even more sorrows yet to bear.

Why will anyone be astonished at the power of Mary now in Heaven? Did she not well earn it on the first Good Friday in the midst of all the desolation of Calvary when Jesus was put to death as a criminal. Mary was not ashamed of Jesus nor did she desert Him, even though His best friends were scandalized at His death and at His being classed among public criminals. Mary was not ashamed of Jesus, and Jesus is now not ashamed of her. Mary did not refuse the Cross, nor did she ask to be relieved from it. She stood by Jesus in His shame and ignominy, and she is now reaping the reward of her generosity. On that day Mary was spared nothing. Mary could realize from the deep expression of anguish on the countenance of Jesus that He was, like herself, suffering the interior trial of abandonment. This, added to His bodily sufferings, was the final drop in the cup of anguish put to the lips of Mary. She had to drink the cup of sorrow to the very dregs. Jesus cries out in the darkness of Good Friday and in the most piteous tones, as of one sinking into unspeakable depths of desolation, "My God, my God, why hast thou forsaken me."

These words rend the heart of Mary in two. They were like the lance which pierced the Heart of Jesus. These words of Jesus first pierced her heart, and this filled up her sufferings to the point when nature, although aided by grace, is scarcely able to bear any more. She now realized what the abandonment of Jesus must have been in addition to His bodily sufferings. She herself had suffered this desolation, but she had never endured the anguish that Jesus now suffered. Jesus had been nailed to the Cross, and yet He uttered no sigh of anguish. He had remained for some time on the Cross, but He does not complain of all He is undergoing for the salvation of souls. But the desolation of being utterly abandoned and forsaken by His Heavenly Father was so great that it almost broke the Sacred Heart, and He uttered this piercing cry of a soul utterly forsaken. His poor dear Mother could give Jesus no comfort, and here she has to stand and do nothing but join her sufferings with those of Jesus for the salvation of souls. At last the sufferings of Jesus come to an end, and He cries out, "Father, into thy hands I commend my spirit," and He dies. Mary heard these last words of Jesus. She heard the words spoken to herself and St. John, and now she is alone. She has been left to the care of the Faithful Disciple.

Jesus by His death gained graces for the Church in her work for the salvation of souls. Mary united her prayers and sufferings with those of Jesus to help in the work of salvation. If we would like to offer our sympathy to Mary for all the agonies of Good Friday, we cannot please this dear Mother better than by offering—like her—our sufferings and crosses for the conversion of sinners. Mary gave a message to all the faithful when she appeared at Lourdes and told the little shepherdess to pray for sinners. We will make the best of all returns to Jesus and Mary if we will only aid them by our prayers in the work of salvation. If only those who are burdened with sorrows and cares would have recourse to Mary, she would obtain grace to enable them to sanctify themselves by their sufferings, and she would console them in their trials. By her sufferings on Calvary she has gained the power to help us in all needs of soul and body.

> Mother of God, from out thy heart
> Our Saviour fashioned His;
> The fountains of the Precious Blood
> Rose in thy depths of bliss.
>
> Mother of God, He broke thy heart,
> That it might wider be,
> That in the vastness of its love
> There might be room for me.

Von Ach

THE CRUCIFIXION

Janssens

SIXTH SORROW—JESUS IS TAKEN DOWN FROM THE CROSS

CHAPTER XIII

The Taking Down from the Cross

JESUS had died and the work of redemption had been completed. While He was hanging on the Cross before His death, He was left desolate and He seemed to have no friends. He had scarcely breathed His last sigh when two holy men, Joseph of Arimathea and Nicodemus, were inspired by God to take care of His dead body. These good men take the body of Jesus from the Cross, and they bury the body in the tomb which Joseph of Arimathea had prepared for himself. We see here how God shows His care for those who suffer for Him and help in the salvation of souls. They may seem to be forgotten, even by God, but this apparent forgetfulness is only an act of love on the part of God to enable them to gain all the merit of their sufferings. God inspires holy souls to help them in all their trials.

The body, when taken down from the Cross, was placed in the arms of His Holy Mother. This was another grief of Mary. If she had not fully realized the extent of the sufferings of Jesus before this, she can now do so. She examines the wounds in the hands and feet, and as she does so, she sees again in her mental vision the tortured countenance of Jesus as the nails were driven through those hands which had so often been raised in benediction. These holy men thought it would console Mary to press the dead body of Jesus to her bosom, but they little knew that the sight of the wounds would pierce again her heart with so many swords of anguish and sorrow. She looks at the sweet Countenance and impresses upon the Sacred Face the kiss of a heartbroken Mother. She sees the marks of the cruel thorns which were driven deep into the Sacred Brow. She goes over in her mind what terrible pain and what depth of humiliation the

93

cruel Crowning of Thorns was to her Jesus. But she looks into that sweet dead face of Jesus. The look of anguish and the depth of suffering which even in death were impressed on the Divine Countenance of Jesus was like another sword of desolation piercing the sweet heart of Mary. Mary was glad in the depth of her soul that Jesus had suffered so much and had completed His great work, but alas, her sufferings were not yet over. Her eyes catch a glimpse of the marks of the Scourging. She sees that the flesh has been torn away, and her maternal hands can feel the bones laid bare by the cruelty and brutality of those half-drunken soldiers. She hears again the scourges hissing through the air and falling on the back and shoulders of her Divine Son. She kisses the marks of the wounds, and she prays with all the fervor of her soul that the sufferings of Jesus may not be in vain but may be efficacious in the remission of sins. Even here Mary does not withdraw the sacrifice she once made in offering her Son to the Eternal Father as a Victim for the sins of the world. Jesus came to the world specially for the work of Redemption, but by the offering made by Mary in giving Jesus as a Victim, her own merit was increased, and her prayers and sufferings, united to those of Jesus, were very powerful in obtaining grace for the salvation of souls.

What an example for parents is Mary! Some parents will give their children to God in the fervor of their early years, but later on, when they feel the loneliness of old age or when sorrow crosses their path, they withdraw part of the sacrifice and sigh for the love of their dear ones. Mary never took back the least part of her offering to God, although her heart was breaking with sorrow. If parents would only, like Mary, offer their sufferings in union with those of Jesus on Calvary for the conversion of sinners, they would increase their merits and do much for Our Lord's interests by helping, by their patience in suffering, with the works of salvation. They would also obtain grace for their own children to sanctify themselves in their works for God's glory. This renewal of the offering of all our past sorrows and sacrifices to God for the conversion of sinners pleases the Sacred Heart and consoles the sweet Jesus for the want of generosity among so many of His lukewarm and weak-hearted friends. As Mary examined the wounds on the dead body of Jesus, she offered each suffering of Jesus for the salvation of souls. She pleaded as a mother has the right to plead who gives up her child to God. She asks that those sufferings of her dear Son, in view of all the sorrows which had overwhelmed her own heart and all the agonies endured by Jesus, might be accepted for the welfare of the Church and for the salvation of all the nations throughout the world.

The taking down from the Cross brings to our minds another devotion which concerns each one of us. The body of Jesus in the arms of Mary is one of the best ways of representing Jesus in our souls in Holy Communion. During the Holy Sacrifice of the Mass, we ought to stand with Mary at the foot of the Cross, and at the moment of Consecration we should picture Jesus being raised up on the Cross, and as we stand with Mary, we should allow the precious Blood to drop into our souls to wash away every stain of sin. Like Mary also, we should pray and offer the sufferings of Jesus for the conversion of sinners and for the spread of the Faith and for the welfare of the Church. At the moment of receiving Holy Communion, let us receive the dear body of Jesus into our souls as Our Lady received it when taken down from the Cross. It is at that moment we ought to press Jesus to our hearts and pray with all the fervor of our love that Jesus might purify our souls in the Precious Blood. As we examine the wounds in the body of Jesus, we can, like Mary, pray for the salvation of those poor unfortunate souls who will not accept the blessings of Jesus nor obey the teachings of the Church. We ought to pray that the

Church may be preserved from the ravages of heresy, for which Jesus suffered so much.

Although Holy Communion resembles very much the taking down from the Cross, yet when we now receive Jesus in the Holy Communion, we must remember that He is now living, and our prayers will on that account be all the more efficacious. Mary prayed when she held the dear but wounded and dead body of Jesus. In Holy Communion we have the living but wounded body of Jesus, and Jesus now prays for us and with us. When will we ever learn to value the few moments after Holy Communion when we have Jesus all to ourselves and when we have at our disposal all the merits of the Passion. Those few moments are so often allowed to pass without making the profit from them that we ought to make. Again, why will so many shorten their few moments of thanksgiving after Holy Communion when each second is so precious for eternity and for souls? The sweet Heart of Jesus is saddened when He finds souls so engrossed in worldly and unimportant cares that they seem to have no time to give to Him. In Holy Communion Jesus comes simply laden with graces, but so few souls are capable of receiving them.

Some may perhaps suggest that Jesus could bestow these graces on souls without any necessity for prayer. Yes, Jesus fills the soul in Holy Communion with all the graces she is capable of receiving, but prayer removes the obstacles to grace, and by eliciting acts of sorrow for sin and acts of love and confidence, we prepare our souls for the blessings of Jesus. In the midst of worldly distractions Jesus cannot speak to the soul. After Holy Communion, Jesus loves to have a few moments of sweet intercourse with us. This is the best of all times to prove our sincere love for Jesus by making fervent acts of reparation and of thanksgiving for all His goodness and His sufferings. The Sacred Heart of Jesus is so often made sorrowful by the coldness of so many who are supposed to be His friends. How Jesus is consoled when we give Him a welcome into our souls in the Sacrament of His love! Very, very few ever think of the love of Jesus in His Passion and Death. Jesus gave the very last drop of His Precious Blood and suffered tortures of mind and body to expiate for sin and to give to souls the merits of His sufferings. Yet the majority of people will pass by, just as they did on the first Good Friday, and pay no heed to all the pleadings of His Passion and to all the words of forgiveness spoken on behalf of His executioners. The Holy Sacrifice of the Mass brings the fruits of the Passion of Jesus to all parts of the world, and Holy Communion brings not only the fruits of the Passion but the very body of Jesus, which actually suffered for us, into the soul of each of the faithful. As Mary received Jesus in her arms with all the tenderness of a mother's love, so ought we to receive Jesus in Holy Communion, and in this way we will make the best of all returns to both Jesus and Mary for all they have suffered for us. When Mary received the dead body of Jesus, she pressed it to her heart and she joined her sufferings with those that Jesus endured for the salvation of souls.

Mary is now highest in Heaven because she suffered more than any of the saints and because her soul, being so filled with grace, made her sufferings so efficacious for souls. When we have followed Mary up the long hill of Calvary and have stood with her for three hours at the foot of the Cross and have seen her with the lifeless and mangled body of Jesus in her arms, we have no cause to wonder at her present exaltation. She has well earned all her glory, and she now makes good use of all the powers she possesses for the assistance of the poor and afflicted. Oh, how good and sweet is this most amiable Mother! How her sweet and maternal heart yearns for the salvation of souls! How much she will do for her children or for all who approach her! As she carried the body of Jesus in her arms, she can lay claim to all the sufferings of Jesus, for she has followed Him all through His Passion and has remained to the very end. Who will ever describe the extent of her grief or her desolation as she followed Jesus through all the stages of His Crucifixion. We may see this sweet Mother with the holy women going up the hill of Calvary following Jesus. The lips of the Mother of God are almost of a deathly blue; her cheeks are as pale as death; her eyes are red with weeping; her hands are trembling with grief and desolation; and her heart and soul are immersed in a sea of sorrow. Oh, who will not shed tears of compassion at the sight of this poor sweet heartbroken Mother. She whose whole life had been spent in acts of kindness and charity and who never had a single thought of self all through her life has now to tread this path of thorns in the midst of the jeers of the thoughtless and cruel multitude. Yet in the midst of all her anguish, she prays for the conversion of sinners and obtains numerous graces for the Church and for souls. Oh, may this sorrowful and most sweet Mother protect her children from all the wiles of the devil and may she receive their souls on the shores of eternity and press them to her maternal heart as she pressed the dear dead body of Jesus when it was taken down from the Cross.

> Oh, ye who pass along the way,
>   All joyous, where with grief I pine,
> In pity pause a while and say,
>   Was ever sorrow like to mine?
>
> See lying here before my eyes
>   This body, bloodless, bruised, and torn;
> Alas, it is my Son who dies—
>   Of love deserving, not of scorn.
>
> He is my God, and since that night
>   When first I saw His Infant grace,
> My soul has feasted on the light,
>   The beauty of that heavenly face.

Ah, loving souls, love; love that God
  Who all inflamed with love expires.
On you His life He has bestowed;
  Your love is all that He desires.

Janssens

SEVENTH SORROW—JESUS IS LAID IN THE SEPULCHER

CHAPTER XIV

The Burial of Jesus

THE DEAD body of Jesus is taken from the arms of Mary and placed in the tomb. Mary follows the funeral procession. What a sad procession and how little of worldly pomp or external show there is about it. The heart of the Mother of God is ready to burst with grief after all the agonies of the Crucifixion, and now in sorrow she follows the holy men who are carrying the body to its resting place. The Sepulcher is opened, and the lifeless body of Jesus is placed within it. Before the stone is placed over the door of the Sepulcher, Mary gives one final glance of love at the sweet and tortured countenance of Jesus and impresses on it her last kiss of love, and then with St. John and the holy women she withdraws for the night. This first Good Friday night was a terrible and desolate night for Mary.

We have sometimes seen a broken-hearted wife or mother bearing up during the illness of her dear one, and even during the time of death showing forth fortitude which surprised all who were standing by. But on the evening after the funeral, when the mind begins to reflect on all the agonies of the death and on the blank created in her life, she views the past and the future, and it is only then that the real grief commences. How often have we seen a widowed mother give expression to her feelings of sadness and desolation by heartfelt sobs and tears and by piteous exclamations of loneliness which would rend the hardest heart with grief and sympathy. Who has not seen strong women bearing up under some heavy cross for some time and then, when the crisis has passed, the suppressed feelings of sorrow burst forth because nature could no longer stand the strain. During the day Mary had followed Jesus up the steep hill of

Calvary. She had most likely been present at the brutal scourging when Jesus was all one wound, from head to foot. She was often on the point of dying with grief, but yet she bore up and united her sufferings with those of Jesus for the salvation of souls. Now she has time to reflect. Jesus is dead and buried. She is now alone. Her mind goes back over all the tortures of the Crucifixion, and she gives vent to her inward sorrow in tears of unutterable anguish. How lonely and desolate she feels during the night of Good Friday, and how St. John and the holy women try to comfort her! But Mary's heart had felt too much suffering to be comforted on this side of eternity.

She never knew how much she loved Jesus until now. All her life, Mary's love for Jesus grew as she grew in age and in grace, but now that He had died, her love increased beyond the bounds of earth, and her separation from Jesus was an unceasing torture. She longed to be with Jesus, and yet she wished to remain on earth to comfort the Apostles. Mary's love for Jesus now was so intense that her whole body was as a consuming fire, and the vehemence of her love gave her no rest day or night for the remainder of her life. The love of Jesus corresponds with the grace possessed by a soul. Mary had followed Jesus through His Passion and had drunk the last drop of the chalice of affliction, and now her soul was immersed in a sea of sorrow and of love. It was really a torture for Mary to be separated now from Jesus. Yet as she had forgotten herself all through life and thought only of Jesus and the good of others, Mary now never once asks to be taken out of the world. Had she done so, she would have taken back some of the sacrifice and would have given something to herself, but Mary had long since learned to forget self.

The essence of all sanctity is to forget self and give all to God and souls. God's will had become for Mary her rule of life. Oh, how she loved God and souls! We never find the love of God separated from zeal for the salvation of souls. If Mary were now to give to any of her children the advice of a mother who loves her child, she would say, "My child, love; love, my child; leave out all thought of self. This is the enemy of all holiness. My dear child as I take thee in my arms and press thee to my heart as I did the Infant Jesus, whom I loved as no mother ever loved her son, I ask you to love deeply and forget yourself." This world is rendered so cold, and souls are lost for the want of love. Mary remained in this world for many years after the Ascension of Jesus. The sorrows of Calvary impressed themselves so indelibly on the soul of Mary that for the rest of her life the sufferings of Jesus never left her mind. She visited the scenes of the Passion, and even when away from Jerusalem, she revisited these scenes and rehearsed them in her mind so much that the dolors of Jesus never ceased to occupy her attention. The sword of Simeon had so pierced her heart that nothing but the sight of Jesus could ever heal it again.

Who will ever describe the influence of Mary upon the Apostles and disciples. Her sweet but sad countenance reflected the depth of suffering she had undergone, but her sweetness was like a perfume which diffused itself on all sides. What comfort she imparted to the first converts and how her holiness diffused itself all around. If we converse with a holy person for some time, we will always feel ourselves influenced by the perfume of his sanctity. The very words and look of a saint convey grace to souls. What then must have been the influence of Mary after the Ascension of Jesus. May we not say that the fervor of the Apostles was largely due to her presence and to the power of her prayers? Before the Descent of the Holy Ghost, Mary remained with the Apostles in prayer. Oh, how she prayed for the success of the Church and for the sanctity of the Apostles! The ten days' preparation for Pentecost were spent in prayer with

Mary, and as a result of this preparation the Holy Ghost distributes His gifts to the Apostles because they were prepared to receive them. Do we not see how the prayers of Mary and her presence with the Apostles did so much to prepare them for the gifts of the first Pentecost.

Jesus by His death gained graces for the salvation of souls, but Jesus has now left these graces in the Church. Jesus still remains with the Church in the Blessed Eucharist and offers in the Sacrifice of the Mass His sufferings and death for the salvation of souls. At the Cross still stands Mary who prays for the salvation of souls. Oh, if we could only realize the power of Mary for the conversion of sinners! Jesus and Mary suffered together all through life. Jesus and Mary are engaged now in keeping souls out of Hell. Jesus and Mary are engaged in raising up saints in the Church who will do much for the sake of the souls for whom they suffered. If we wish to come close to Jesus, our shortest and easiest way is through Mary. She is so close to Jesus now and her power of intercession is so great that she has only to say to Jesus, "Son, this is my child, I give him to you," and at once we are placed within the dear Sacred Heart of Jesus. If we could only have a faint idea of Our Lady's sweetness! Many chosen souls have experienced the sweetness of Mary. This has always been the beginning of a life of sanctity. Listen to the saints of God as they speak of Our Lady. The saints have been specially enlightened by God so that their words are those of souls experienced in the paths of sanctity. These chosen souls never cease to sing the praises of Mary as they grow in devotion to this sweet Mother. The years spent by Mary on this earth after the Crucifixion were years when Mary grew in sanctity and in sweetness.

St. John had the privilege of guarding this sweet Mother after the death of Jesus. In his early days, St. John had been an impetuous Galilean who once wished to call down fire from Heaven to consume those people who would not give Our Lord hospitality. Towards the end of his life, he preached one sermon, and that was, "Children, love one another." He lived to be a great age, and when he was no longer able to go about, he was still preaching this sermon: "My children, love one another." Where did St. John gain his sweetness and love? This was not natural to his impetuous nature. Where did he gain these sentiments of love but from her who is preeminently the Mother of love. Jesus is Love Incarnate. It was love that brought Jesus from Heaven to redeem the world. It is love that keeps Jesus in the Blessed Sacrament. It is love that brings Jesus into our souls in Holy Communion. Mary brings Jesus into our souls in Holy Communion. Mary is the Mother of Jesus and so the Mother of love. Mary is engaged in bringing hearts to love Jesus and to love each other. Oh, the love and the sweetness of this Holy Mother! She may appear to souls sometimes as if she asks too much love and too much for Jesus, but when she is approached, she has the smile of sweetness which at once begets confidence. Her face saddened by the sorrows of Good Friday has still the smile of friendship for all those who will accept her blessings. Never once has Mary been seen but in the smile of friendship and confidence. Her sweet though sometimes sad smile now seems to say to us: "O my child, let me fill you with treasures. How I long to press you to my heart. Have patience and accept my blessings for a few years, and then I will come to bring you to Heaven, where your sorrows will all be over. O my child, do love Jesus! He is now in the Blessed Eucharist, and so many will refuse to love Him, even in the very Sacrament of Love. My child, help Jesus and help me to save souls by our prayers for the conversion of sinners." The sweet smile which Mary gives to her children in this world enables them to persevere till death in the love and service of Jesus and Mary.

Mary died about twenty-four years after the Ascension

of Jesus. As she grew in grace, her love for God continued to grow. The intensity of her love for God was like a feeling of attraction for the object beloved, so strong that it consumed every earthly feeling. As her love for God grew, so did her love for her neighbor. But Mary's love for others was not as the love of most people, who love others generally for selfish motives. Most people, and even good people, love others and wish for others' company because this will bring some happiness to themselves. Mary had long ago forgotten all about self. She even forgot all about her own soul. She had no time left for the thought of self. All her time was given to the love of God and to the work of the salvation of souls. She prayed very much for the welfare of the Church and she prayed that the faithful, till the End of Time, might persevere and that the Church might triumph over all heresy and schism. How she prayed for the unity of the Church and for the destruction of all heresies! We may now see the reason behind all the hatred of heretics for Mary. Her prayers have rendered them powerless to destroy the Church of God.

At last the vehemence of the love of Mary is so great that nature can no longer contain her soul, and so her pure soul, unsullied by the least breath of sin, takes its flight to God. O dear sweet Mother Mary, teach us true love of Jesus. Teach us to forget self and give all to Jesus and to souls. Teach us the worthlessness of all that this passing world contains. Bestow upon us thy sweet smile of love, which gives confidence in the midst of trials. O dear Mother, defend the seamless garment of the Church and keep out the wolves of heresy. Oh, may devotion to thee be the mark of future ages, for devotion to thee, O Mary, is the best sign of holiness and the best guarantee of perseverance.

What a sea of tears and sorrow
  Did the soul of Mary toss
To and fro upon its billows
  While she wept her bitter loss,
In her arms her Jesus holding,
  Torn so newly from the Cross.

Gentle Mother, we beseech thee,
  By thy tears and troubles sore,
By the death of thy dear Offspring,
  By the bloody wounds He bore,
Touch our hearts with that true sorrow
  Which afflicted thee of yore.

OUR LADY OF LOURDES

CHAPTER XV

Our Lady of Lourdes

IT WOULD seem that all the extraordinary ways of bring-ing souls to Heaven have their origin in the mind of the Mother of God. The Sacred Heart devotion was taught by Jesus, but this is only an aspect of the personal love of Jesus for souls and a means of increasing devotion to Jesus in the Blessed Sacrament. When we consider those devotions which are quite outside the ordinary channels of grace, we can trace then practically all to the zeal of Mary for the salvation of souls. Mary has often appeared in this world and has made known to souls many of the secrets of the kingdom of God, and she has inaugurated many works and has done very much to help the Church in her mission of carrying the fruits of Redemption to mankind. What a blessing that the Church has the help and the counsel of Our Lady at all times! In the first years of the Church's existence, Mary was left in the world to help the Apostles in their guiding the infant Church, and since her Assumption into Heaven, she has returned at different periods and has appeared at different places to help the Church in her divine mission.

The greatest manifestation of the power and goodness of Mary took place at Lourdes in France a little over half a century ago. [*That is, 1858. This book was written prior to the apparitions at Fatima—May 13, 1917 to October 13, 1917. —Editor.*] Mary appeared there to a little peas-ant girl, Bernadette Soubirous, whose parents were poor in worldly goods and were of little account in the eyes of the world. Since that time this little town has become, after Rome, the center of the religious life of the world and the place chosen by God to manifest His power and wisdom. Miracles have been worked at Lourdes during all these years, and these have been so astonishing that they have attracted the notice of the whole world. We see the goodness of Mary in working her miracles so profusely and so publicly that all those who wish to know the Truth can here have a proof of the divinity of the Catholic Church. The zeal of this sweet Mother for the salvation of souls is so great that she has chosen this place and has made it such a center of religious activity that it cannot escape the notice of the whole world. The miracles are so great that they must attract the notice of all thinking men, and in her goodness Mary has left to the world this proof of the supernatural character of the Church. How we ought to give perpetual and never-ending thanks to Our Lady for her goodness in selecting this little town to prove to all that the Catholic Church is the One, True Church and for performing so many miracles as a proof of the Church's divinity!

When Mary appeared to Bernadette, she gave her some messages for herself and she gave her others for the public. It is such a pity that these messages of Our Lady have not been promulgated throughout the world. By promulgation we mean in this connection being acted upon and explained in such a way that they will form a part of the lives of the faithful. Our Lady has one chief object in all her apparitions, and that is the sanctification and salvation of souls. The curing of bodily diseases is not the chief end of Lourdes. This is merely a perpetual proof of Mary's power and a standing and clear manifestation of the Catholic Church. The salvation of one single soul is of more importance in the eyes of Our Lady than the healing of all the diseases of all the bodies that have ever existed. A few years of suffering is very little for an eternity of happiness, and in most cases suffering and sorrow are the easiest roads to holiness and to the taking of our hearts from the passing affairs of this earth. To prove that Mary's design at Lourdes was the sanctification of souls, she did not cure Bernadette, her favorite child, but promised that she would make her happy, not in this world, but in the next. Mary said to the little shepherdess: "Penance, penance, penance." This thrice repeated request for penance, during a time when penitential works were scoffed at, was intended to teach once more to the world the necessity of self-denial in the great work of salvation. It has been fashionable to scoff at penitential works in years past, and even among the faithful the necessity of penance has not been appreciated.

The whole truth is that penance or self-denial is the very essence of the spiritual life. The supernatural not only rises above but generally requires the overcoming of nature or the fighting against our natural inclinations. It is not that these inclinations are always bad in themselves, but they are very liable to be abused unless nature is raised up or aided by the grace of God. Penance does not mean self-denial for its own sake, as this is not necessarily supernatural. True penance means turning towards God by works of self-denial. What Our Lady intended to teach to the world was that the performance of natural good works alone was of no value for securing the supernatural rewards of Heaven. She in other words wished to teach the necessity of supernatural good works for salvation. It has been a common saying by those who perform no supernatural good works that they are as good as those who do works of penance and self-denial. When a priest has asked a person if he prays or hears Mass on Sunday, the answer often has been that he is as good as those who go to Mass, and strange to say this answer has set many people thinking. Very many have lost the Faith through associating with such people who have no faith and have no idea of the supernatural. The reply to the objection that those who go to Mass and pray are no better than those who do not go is simply that those who do not go to Mass and who do not pray may be as good as those who go, as far as natural good works are concerned, but that natural good works will bring forth no reward for eternity. Supernatural rewards or the eternal vision of God can only be secured by the grace of God, which is gained by supernatural good works. When Our Lord told the people to lay up treasures in Heaven, He meant that they ought to sanctify their souls by obtaining God's grace, which is obtained by the performance of supernatural good works. When a person is baptized, he receives a new spiritual existence, which raises him up to a new state of life and makes him a partaker even of the Divine Nature by the reason of the presence of Sanctifying Grace. This grace is increased by supernatural good works and by feeding the soul with heavenly food. Just as the natural life requires food so does the supernatural, and the supernatural food of the soul is nothing less than the Body and Blood of Jesus in Holy Communion. Again, as the human mind requires to be nourished with knowledge in order to be properly developed, so does the intellect raised up by grace require the supernatural knowledge of Christian doctrine. The will must perform good actions in the natural order if we wish to develop our faculties; and in the same way, if we wish to be supernaturally developed, our wills must be trained to the performance of supernatural good works. All supernatural works mean some self-denial because these go beyond the powers of nature, and when we perform penitential works, we secure grace and thereby gain merit for eternity.

We need not go into details here about the works of penance which Our Lady would wish us to perform, but the ordinary good actions performed for a good intention will be within the reach of all and will be sufficient to secure salvation. Frequent prayer and especially morning and evening prayers said with some fervor are very meritorious works and obtain abundant graces for the performances of good actions and for the avoidance of sin. Hearing Mass and going frequently to Holy Communion, especially every Sunday, are also very penitential and supernatural works, and the nourishment of our souls by frequent and if possible daily Communion will not only keep alive the state of grace but will increase the grace in our souls and help us to avoid sin. The offering of all our works and sufferings in the spirit of penance for the love of God will be a perpetual source of grace, and if we preserve patience under trials for Our Lord's sake, we are imitating Jesus in His Passion and Death.

Our Lady also said to Bernadette, "Pray for sinners." This is the most charitable of all works and will gain for us the everlasting rewards of Heaven. Charity, or love for our neighbor for Our Lord's sake, is so pleasing to God that it is Our Lord's own special commandment. "This is my commandment, that you love one another." This charity, to be true, must be supernatural or must have God for its motive. We must love our neighbor for Our Lord's sake. When we assist the poor or the oppressed, we gain great graces and please Our Lord very much. To feed the hungry and to console the afflicted are works dear to the Heart of Jesus, and for these Jesus has promised an everlasting reward. Even a cup of cold water given for the love of Jesus will be rewarded eternally. But in feeding the hungry we merely have compassion on our neighbor's body, and we may not in any way assist his soul, although we will be rewarded for our charity if we assist our neighbor in his temporal needs for the love of God. If by our charity we can save even one soul from Hell, we will do an action more pleasing to God than if we feed millions of starving human beings. Yet Our Lady had good reason to give the message to pray for sinners because so very very few have any zeal for the salvation of souls. We have many ways of helping in the salvation of souls, and the first way is to pray and offer our little sacrifices for the conversion of sinners. We could offer up Mass or Holy Communion, and we could pray at Mass and after Holy Communion for the conversion of sinners. We could offer our little crosses and sufferings for this intention. The saints reached great heights of glory because they prayed and offered all their sufferings for the conversion of sinners and for the spread of the Faith. We may feel that we have been offended, and we may be anxious for an opportunity for revenge. In such a case, if we will pray for patience and offer the act of forgiveness for the salvation of souls, we will satisfy for our own sins and we will gain very many graces for the conversion and salvation of others. We may be asked for an alms for the spread of the Faith, and if we deprive ourselves of some luxury in order to perform this act of supernatural charity and offer the sacrifice for sinners, we will do much for God's glory. Besides prayers for sinners, we can aid in the salvation of souls by our zeal for the salvation of our neighbor. We can entice others to prayer and to the avoidance of sin. We can support all good works for the welfare of the Church and help in the works for the propagation of the Faith. The best of all means will be to give our lives to God in the religious life or the priesthood, where we will devote our whole lives to prayer, penance and work for the salvation of souls. The apostolic life is a life of penance for souls, and those who embrace this life are virtually assured of the everlasting crown of glory and of special honor at the Last Day. All can do Our Lady's wish by at least praying frequently for sinners.

THE IMMACULATE CONCEPTION

THE MOTHER OF GOD

CHAPTER XVI

The Month of Mary

WHEREVER we see an increase of devotion to Mary, there also we notice a greater love for Jesus. In the history of those countries which preserved the Faith in spite of all persecutions of heretics and in the face of all the fury of Hell itself, we notice that devotion to Our Lady was a characteristic of the people. In the lives of the greatest saints, we notice Mary interwoven with Jesus, just as she was in this world. The early Church triumphed over her enemies, and the Apostles made great progress, notwithstanding their former slowness of understanding. This is attributed of course to the gifts of the Holy Ghost at Pentecost, but perhaps if we could lift the veil that separates time from eternity, we would see that Mary's prayers and her counsel during her years on earth after the Ascension had very much to do with the success of the Apostles, as she it was who by her prayers for the Apostles paved the way for the infusion of these gifts. It would be difficult to find a single saint, of whose life history has a record, without noticing how Mary used her influence and her sweetness to entice the soul to great sanctity and union with God.

It may be that Mary is now so anxious for the salvation of souls that, when she sees a soul likely to correspond with God's grace, she bestows upon it some mark of her affection, and henceforth that soul is sure of her special protection. How many can trace the seeds of their vocation to some little act of devotion to Mary in their early years, and how many souls on the brink of eternity would confess that they owed very much of their graces and their hope of salvation to this most sweet Mother. It would seem that the occupation of Jesus and Mary is now to save souls. Jesus does this now principally through the Holy Eucharist, but Mary helps her Divine Son in the salvation of souls. Once Mary bestows her sweet smile upon anyone, then there is no need to fear about the salvation of such a privileged soul. Mary loves her children and guards them with far more care and far more affection than any earthly mother could love her child. If only the sweetness of Mary were understood, she would have all the souls in the world at her feet, and she would bring them all to the feet of her sweet Son Jesus.

The month of May has been set apart by the Church for the special devotion to the Mother of God. This whole month has been given to Mary. It has recently been called the month of Our Lady of the Blessed Sacrament, and the 13th of May has been set apart for the special feast of Our Lady of the Blessed Sacrament. Wherever we find a tabernacle erected for Jesus or an altar for the offering of the Sacrifice of the Mass, there you will always find an altar erected to Mary. The Church will not separate Mary from Jesus, and around monasteries and convents we will always find the statue of Mary inviting her children to go in and pay a visit to her Jesus. The Blessed Sacrament is the greatest of all the treasures in the Church. It is the source of practically all graces and the consolation of the faithful in this land of exile. We must thank Mary for the Blessed Eucharist. Mary gave Jesus to the world. She offered Him in the Temple on the feast of the Presentation, and she consummated or fulfilled that offering on the first Good Friday.

Jesus left Himself in the world in the Blessed Eucharist, but as we must thank Mary for giving us Jesus, so we must thank her for the great treasure of the Blessed Eucharist. The title of the month of Our Lady of the Blessed Sacrament is appropriate also for another reason. We always notice that those who are Mary's children and those who give her some marks of their affection are also known to be specially devoted to the Blessed Eucharist. It would seem that Mary brings her children to this source of all grace and sanctification, and in the same way Jesus wishes that those who are devoted to Him should also be devoted to His own sweet Mother Mary. We would expect this on many grounds. A mother wishes to introduce her son to all her friends and so does the son wish to have his mother known to and respected by those whom he loves. Jesus and Mary are so closely united that those who are devoted to the One soon become acquainted with the other. We need the assistance and the prayers of Mary if we wish to gain great and close union with Jesus, and if we are the children of this sweet Mother, she will soon lead us to the source of all graces—the Blessed Sacrament.

The month of Our Lady of the Blessed Sacrament, or the month of May, has been given over to public honor to this sweet Mother of Jesus in many countries. Processions and banners, with hymns and Rosaries, have been the usual scenes during the month of May in Catholic countries. These external manifestations, besides their intrinsic value as marks of love and affection for Mary, are also useful for many other reasons. They entice people towards prayer, and once a soul knows how to pray and once she has a love of prayer, then her salvation is secure. Prayer means almost everything in the work of salvation because if we pray, we will obtain grace, and our minds will be enlightened to do all God wishes us to do. These manifestations of our love for Mary, with their processions and hymns, are also useful to entice all, but especially young people, from frequenting places which might lead them into sin. The great cause of the loss of souls is not that people are not warned about the dangers of sin and the consequences of sin. There is generally quite enough preaching and teaching about sin and not sufficient knowledge of the importance of securing grace. Sin is not avoided by being warned of its consequence. The best way to avoid sin is to entice people towards goodness and to give them plenty of scope in a good direction for all their energies. Young people especially need to be doing something, and it is all a matter of keeping them doing something good. They will want some company, and it is all important to give them good company. A great source of loss to souls is reading bad books and papers. Yet the reading of books and papers could be made use of to stir up lofty sentiments and to convey Christian knowledge to those who are just at the critical stage of life. It is such a pity that parents and teachers do not give young people an outlet for their energies and entice them to noble actions and stir up all their enthusiasm for everything that is great and noble. Good literature is at the present age the chief infallible remedy against the corruption of worldly society and the only sure way to counteract the evil influences of a secular press.

St. Philip Neri introduced many processions into Italy in order to entice the young from the pagan festivities which were carried on during his time. He was so enlightened by God that he was able to realize that the whole secret of the salvation of the young was to entice them towards something good and to keep them occupied with good things. He introduced public processions throughout Italy in honor of the Mother of God, and it is remarkable that in spite of all the wiles of the devil, this country could never be captured by the heretics who tried so hard to overthrow the Church. Do we not see here that the devotion to Mary is one of the best safeguards against heresy, schism, and infidelity. The Rosary has been one of the chief safeguards of families in the midst of the corruption of worldliness. In all those countries where the family Rosary is practiced, we see that the Faith is not easily destroyed and that the fervor of the people is handed down from generation to generation.

The month of May is now called the month of Our Lady of the Blessed Sacrament, and as devotion to Mary means increased holiness, so devotion to Jesus in the Blessed

Sacrament will mean the sanctification of the world and the salvation of countless souls. Our Lady is the model of all true adorers of the Blessed Sacrament, as she spent the last year of her life in adoration before Jesus in the Holy Eucharist, and Holy Communion was during those years her principal food. As in the past, it has been usual to honor Mary by external marks of affection, so in the future the honor given to Mary will take on a more interior aspect and will tend more and more towards the sanctification of souls. As we honor Mary by decorating her altars in our homes and by carrying banners in her honor, so in the future will be added to all these the special love of Jesus in the Blessed Sacrament.

The best of all ways to keep a feastday of Mary is to make our hearts on that day a tabernacle for Jesus in Holy Communion. The month of Mary will also be sanctified in the future by a greater love for Jesus in the Blessed Eucharist. If Mary is to have for her special title in ages to come, "Our Lady of the Blessed Sacrament," we must naturally expect that her special month will also be a time of increased love of Jesus in the Holy Eucharist. Mary's children will still erect altars in their homes during Our Lady's month, and the family Rosary will still be recited in the homes of the faithful. These little practices of devotion to Mary have sown the seeds of holiness in families, and the picture of Mary and the devotion to her has sanctified many humble homes and has been one of the best allurements towards a life of virtue and self-denial. The purity and sanctity of millions of families may be traced to these little acts of devotion to Mary, and this childlike trust of Mary's children has been a source of grace and has enticed people to prayer, besides raising their minds towards what is sweet, gracious and noble.

Mary is the model of all true adorers of Jesus, and so we may expect to find Mary's children visiting Jesus in the Tabernacle with far more earnestness than in years past. What a pity to see so many people wasting their time, especially on Saturday and Sunday, in the company of worldlings and in the reading of secular newspapers. During the years after the Ascension of Jesus, Mary was not really absent from her Divine Son. She spent most of her time with Jesus in the Blessed Sacrament. Mary's children will be seen in future years spending, like their Mother, very much time with Jesus before the Tabernacle. Then they will grow in sanctity and in zeal, and Jesus Himself will enlighten their minds and entice them to greater and greater perfection. We pass from Mary to Jesus. Devotion to Mary, devotion to her Rosary, devotion to the Sacred Heart are all roads which lead to Jesus in the Holy Eucharist. May the month of Mary be truly and sincerely devoted to Mary, and may this sweet Mother lead us to the feet of Jesus, and there we shall dwell within the very Heart of God and our faults shall be consumed in the flames of the love of the Sacred Heart.

> Thee, Virgin Mother dearest,
> We greet with gladsome lay
> And haste with flowers fairest
> To crown thee Queen of May.

Bernardino Luini

THE HEAD OF THE VIRGIN

Our Lady of the Blessed Sacrament

CHAPTER XVII

Our Lady of the Blessed Sacrament

W HEN Our Lady was asked by the little shepherdess at Lourdes what was her name, she answered, "I am the Immaculate Conception." Very probably, if she were asked today what title she would prefer, she would answer, "Our Lady of the Blessed Sacrament." This is the most recent of the titles of Mary, and the Holy See has graciously assigned the 13th of May each year for the celebration of this feast. If we examine this latest title of Mary, we cannot fail to be struck by the depth of its meaning and by its power of raising our thoughts to the most sublime and most devotional of all mysteries. When Our Lord revealed to St. Margaret Mary the desire of His Sacred Heart to receive honor and reparation, He also said that this devotion was intended to inflame the hearts of the faithful with love and was to inaugurate a period of fervor in the Church. This Sacred Heart of Jesus now lives in the Blessed Sacrament, and the increase of devotion to the Blessed Sacrament is the chief result of the spread of the devotion to the Sacred Heart of Jesus.

We might say in a few words that all graces at present come from the Blessed Sacrament, and all other devotions in the Church are rather aids or helps towards increased devotion to Our Lord in the Sacrament of His love. During the past few centuries we notice also an increase of devotion to Our Blessed Lady, the Mother of Jesus. The Rosary has been again and again recommended by the Vicar of Christ as a devotion suitable to all ages and all times, but more especially as a family prayer in order to create a supernatural bond in the family and to obtain the protection of the Holy Mother of God on all Christian families. This devotion to the

Mother of God is always accompanied with an increase of devotion to Jesus in the Blessed Sacrament. Devotion to Mary is merely the way or the road to reach Jesus, and the center and source of all graces now is the Holy Eucharist. We see at Lourdes, where the Mother of Jesus is honored, that the devotion to the Blessed Sacrament increases in this center of holiness just in proportion to the increase in devotion to Mary.

We notice during the lifetime of Jesus that Mary was never far from Him. She carried Him as an infant to Egypt. She lived with her Divine Son for thirty years, and during His Public Life she followed Him, although she never appeared in the public eye. At Calvary she stands with Jesus amidst all the insults of the rabble and then receives His dead body from the Cross. After Our Lord's Ascension, Mary received Jesus every day in the Holy Communion, and as the Blessed Sacrament was then reserved in the early churches, which were generally the homes of some of the early Christians, Mary spent most of her days and nights in adoration before the Tabernacle. It is the teaching of the greatest theologians and historians that the Blessed Sacrament was reserved in the early churches of the Christians for the purpose of adoration and for the Viaticum of the sick. It seems indeed strange that this title of Our Lady of the Blessed Sacrament was not given to Mary until the present age, but perhaps in the designs of God as the devotion to the Blessed Sacrament is to be the special activity of the faithful for the future ages, this title of Our Lady of the Blessed Sacrament will surpass all other titles, and be the one by which her devoted children will love to address her in the periods of fervor and sanctity upon which the Church is just now about to enter.

The devotion to the Holy Eucharist is really the center of all other devotions in the Church and the source of practically all graces. The Mass is the renewal of Calvary. Mary stood with Jesus on Calvary and united her sufferings with those of her Son for the salvation of souls. Without the Mass we would be devoid of the chief means of bringing the fruits of the Passion of Jesus to our souls. Certainly we receive great graces in prayer, but it is through the Mass that we are able actually to lay hold of all the treasures of graces which Jesus obtained for us by all His sufferings. When Jesus was dying on the first Good Friday, very many around the Cross received the grace of the True Faith, and through the prayers of Jesus and Mary, thousands were saved, either through the graces received on that day or at the subsequent preaching of the Apostles. The Centurion, the Good Thief, and very many of the Jews and the soldiers confessed the divinity of Jesus and received the gifts of faith and redemption by their presence on that day.

The Mass is a renewal of the first Good Friday. In His excessive love, Jesus instituted the Blessed Eucharist in order to bring the fruits of Redemption throughout the whole world, so that those who hear Mass in any part of the whole world may receive the gifts of grace and faith which were bestowed upon those who were around the Cross on the first Good Friday. Wherever the Mass is offered, it brings the blessings gained by Our Lord to the souls of all the faithful and to the suffering souls in Purgatory, just as the sufferings of Jesus benefited others besides those who were present at His death; but only those around the Cross gained those special graces which were bestowed only on that day. We see this in the case of the Good Thief and the Centurion. Others who were not present and the faithful of all ages obtained the fruits of the sufferings of Jesus principally through the Sacrifice of the Mass. "Do this," says Jesus, "in commemoration of Me." The Apostles and their successors carried out this command of Our Lord, and now we have fulfilled the prophecy of Malachy, who made known that the Sacrifice of the New Law would be offered in every place from the rising to the setting of the sun.

The Sacrifice of the Mass not only renews the Sacrifice of Calvary, but we are now even more privileged than those who were present at the death of Jesus. In addition to all the merits of the Passion of Jesus, we can now receive the Sacred Body of Jesus in Holy Communion. When we receive Our Lord in Holy Communion, we gain all the fruits of the sufferings of Jesus that our souls are capable of receiving. In the early Church, after the Descent of the Holy Ghost, the faithful were accustomed to receive Holy Communion as often as they were present at the Holy Sacrifice, and it was then recognized that without Holy Communion the graces of the Mass would not be complete for the individual soul. This custom of receiving Jesus daily in Holy Communion must have been taught by Our Lord Himself, because the Apostles and Evangelists speak frequently of the "breaking of bread," and this, according to commentators, refers to Holy Communion.

It is not known with certainty how long Our Lady lived in this world after the Ascension. Suarez and the majority of the early Fathers are of the opinion that Mary lived twenty-four years after the Ascension of Jesus. During these years she was occupied in consoling and instructing the Apostles and making known the great events that took place at Nazareth during the thirty years of the Hidden Life. She aided the faithful by her counsels and brought to them grace by her very presence, and when she spoke, it seemed that the sweetness and calmness of her soul diffused themselves all around. But during these years Mary was growing in grace, and this time was given to her that she might increase in love and in beauty of soul by every action and by every desire of her heart. Already she was so filled with grace that the least action performed by her raised her up in sanctity much more than ever her actions during the mortal life of Jesus. The reason for this is simple. Mary was growing in holiness every moment of her life, and as she grew older, her holiness surpassed that of all the faithful on earth and all the saints in Heaven put together. This meant that the least action of Mary, on account of the high state of grace in her soul, was valuable beyond the actions of others because the grace of the latter was so small in comparison with that of Mary. During all these years Mary grew in grace and in love principally by her devotion to the Blessed Eucharist. Her daily Communions united her to Jesus much more closely than she was united to Him during the thirty years at Nazareth.

Jesus wished His Holy Mother to be as near to Himself for eternity as it is possible for a soul to be, and in the filial love of His Sacred Heart He left Mary in the world for many years after His Ascension. As Mary was nourished every day by the Heavenly Food of the Sacred Body of Jesus, her soul was more and more adorned with all gifts and was raised higher and higher in love and sanctity, so that at last the vehemence of her love burst asunder the cords that tied her to earth, and she took her flight to the bosom of God. Mary might have gone to Heaven with Jesus at the Ascension, but then her sanctity would not have been complete. We do not mean to say that Mary had lost any grace up to that time, because she fully cooperated and made full use of every grace during the whole period of her earthly existence, but the years after the Ascension were intended to raise her up to heights of holiness unheard of before. She was to acquire this extraordinary and surpassing glory through the Holy Eucharist. The daily Communion of Mary was, towards the end of her life, practically her only food, and with each Communion her love for Jesus increased with a rapidity that cannot be measured in human language.

Mary spent the years after the Ascension of Jesus in divine contemplation before the Tabernacle. This was her chief occupation, although she was often interrupted in her adoration, owing to the members who sought her aid. St. Ignatius of Antioch wrote to her asking her to assist him in the struggles that he had to undergo for the Faith. She replied that she would soon visit him at Antioch with St. John. We see again the tender heart of Mary and how sweet she is to all who approach her or seek her aid.

The Blessed Sacrament is now the food of our souls, just as natural food preserves the life of the body. Our Lady's chief occupation now is to help Jesus in the salvation of souls, and we notice that she entices her children towards the Heavenly Food of Holy Communion, and she brings them to Jesus when they are in trouble or sorrow. Mary's children are sometimes anxious to show their love for her, and they will manifest their affection for this tender mother by many external marks of homage. What Mary regards most is the interior purity of heart. This sweet mother was the purest of all God's creatures. To the pure of heart alone will Jesus and Mary communicate their secrets. Purity of heart and purity of intention are best secured by being nourished by the heavenly food of the Holy Eucharist. Mary spent all her spare time, after Our Lord's Ascension, before the Tabernacle in loving converse with Jesus. During these years she gained grace after grace by her prayers and by her devotion to Jesus in the Blessed Sacrament. If we wish to please Mary, we have only to imitate her in her love for Jesus. Mary loves pure souls. Purity is preserved through the Blessed Eucharist. Mary wishes her children to sanctify themselves every day as she did by daily Communion and by adoration and prayer before Jesus in the Tabernacle. May the title of Our Lady of the Blessed Sacrament be properly understood by all the faithful, and then we will soon find the Church producing a harvest of saints greater than in any previous age of her existence.

Sweet Sacrament of Peace,
  Dear home of every heart,
Where restless yearnings cease
  And sorrows all depart.
Here in Thine ear, all trustfully,
  We tell our tale of misery,
Sweet Sacrament of Peace.

OUR LADY HELP OF CHRISTIANS

CHAPTER XVIII

Our Lady Help of Christians

HOLY Simeon foretold that Our Lord would be a sign of contradiction, and this prophecy has been fulfilled, not only during the time of Our Lord's mortal life, but also in every century of the life of His Church. Our Lord's kingdom was in this world but not of the world, and so it followed that the world hated and detested Christ. In the same way, the world hates the Church because she is not of the world and because she opposes the world in its sinful course to final perdition. By the world in this connection, we mean those people who think only of this world and act as if there were no other world and no Redemption by the sufferings of Christ. The world means those people who either ignore or oppose Christ and His Church.

The Church will have to fight against enemies from within and without, but when she fights, she uses the weapons which Christ used. These weapons are meekness, patience, prayer, charity and fortitude, and with these she conquers all her enemies. It is wrong to blame the enemies of the Church for all the trouble in the world. Unfortunately, the Church has often to bewail the ingratitude and waywardness of her own children. When people commit sin, they bring punishment upon themselves by their very own sins, although they may think that by following their evil inclinations they will secure happiness. They may enjoy a false peace and security for a time, but just as surely as sin is committed, so surely will it be punished, and the very wrong-doing will be used as an instrument or a scourge for their correction. When we see whole nations being punished by wars and bloodshed, we may conclude that their punishment was brought upon themselves by their forgetfulness of God.

The Commandments of God are intended for our benefit, and if they are broken, we injure ourselves. Our Lord
begs of us to love Him and to keep His Commandments
because He loves us so much and only wishes to see us
happy. We must not forget that Our Divine Lord and the
saints suffered very much, but their sufferings were to
expiate the sins of others. As a general rule, all suffering
in nations or in individuals comes from disobedience to
God. The Psalmist says, "Before I was humbled, I sinned,"
and this is the general rule in all punishment and in all
humiliation. The sufferings are in accordance with the
sin committed. How often do we see people turning away
from God in order to please their neighbor, and after a
little we see these same neighbors being used as instruments for the punishment of their former so-called
friends.

Very much of the persecution of the Church arises from
the malice of the devil and of wicked men, but very often
also the sufferings of the Church are caused by the sins
of her own children. God permits these sufferings to befall the Church also for the sanctification of souls and
to give the faithful an opportunity of expiating their sins
by their patience under persecution. The Church also
wishes her devout children to sanctify themselves still
more by their sufferings so as to gain the everlasting
crown of glory and to obtain by their fervent prayers and
by their patience grace for the salvation of others. Our
Divine Lord in the Garden of Gethsemane suffered great
interior anguish of soul, and His agony was so terrible
that blood flowed from His body and fell down to the
ground. This terrible mental torture was caused principally by the ingratitude of those for whom He was doing
so much. Our Lord foresaw the sins of the world with
all their hideousness and deformity, and He foresaw the
base ingratitude of those upon whom He lavished all the
treasures of His Sacred Heart, and this detestable self-
ishness and ingratitude were the chief causes of the

torrent of sorrows which overwhelmed the Sacred Heart in the Garden of Olives. The sins of the world have often brought terrible punishments upon its own head, and the ungrateful children of the Church have often been the cause of many and fierce persecution against our sweet Mother the Church, which is the Bride of Christ.

It is most fortunate for the Church and for each individual soul that we have an advocate or a helper in all times of sorrow and trial. The Church calls this advocate the "Help of Christians," and this helper and protector is Mary, Our Mother and the Mother of Jesus. This title of Our Lady, Help of Christians, is perhaps the sweetest and most consoling of all her titles and brings to our mind in an instant what a great source of grace and consolation she is in times of trial or temptation. In the history of the Church, we notice great heresies and persecutions rising up at various times, but we find that as soon as the faithful have recourse to Our Blessed Mother, all the terrors of Hell and all the strength of the wicked are brought to nought. If we take note of those countries which preserved the Faith in spite of all persecutions, we will invariably find that devotion to Mary saved the people from the ravages of heresy and error.

If we again look at those periods in the history of the Church when the powers of Hell seemed about to be victorious, we will find that as soon as the faithful had recourse to Mary, the enemies of the Church were hopelessly defeated. The Albigensian heresy was stopped in its mad career by the devotion to the Rosary of Mary. The suddenness of the destruction of this heresy is perhaps unparalled in history, and yet the devotion to the Holy Rosary was the chief means used to bring back the people to the ways of truth. When the Mohammedan power threatened to overrun Europe, Pope St. Pius V (1566-1572) ordered all the Catholics to unite in prayer to Our Lady and urged the recitation of the Rosary for the success of the Christians, and at the battle of Lepanto

the Turks were driven back for all time. The victory at
Lepanto was wonderful in two ways: The Christians were
fighting against terrible odds, and yet the enemy suffered
a complete defeat and was almost annihilated; the sea
ran red with their blood. At the same time Pope St. Pius
V was miraculously informed of the victory because, at
the very moment when the victory was gained, he suddenly broke off a conversation and said, "Let us give
thanks to God; the victory is won." These words were
taken down and sealed, and a fortnight afterwards a messenger arrived in Rome announcing the glad tidings of
the victory, which took place exactly at the moment when
the Pope uttered the famous words.

It would not be correct to say that Our Lady helps the
Church only in great dangers or at special times. She does
much more than this. She is the advocate of each soul
and the helper in every temptation and the refuge of all
sinners. The poor unfortunate sinner purposely turns
away from God and will not accept His blessings. The
unfortunate creature has turned his back upon God and
has refused all the pleadings of the Sacred Heart. The
sinner is deserted by the angels and the saints, and by
his own act he has deprived himself of God's blessings.
If he would only turn to Our Lord, he would be received
with open arms, but instead of returning to the sweet
and merciful Jesus, the poor sinner too often wanders
away farther and farther. The sinner has left the sweet
embrace of Jesus. He has deserted his father's house and
in his terrible plight he seems hopelessly lost. Oh, what
a misfortune it would be for the unfortunate sinner if
he were forgotten by all the court of Heaven, but he is
not forgotten. The sweet Mother Mary will never desert
the sinner, even till the very last moment of his life. She
is the hope of the hopeless, and she still clings to the
poor sinner and invites him to return to the merciful arms
of Jesus. Oh yes, she is the Star of Hope, and as soon
as the sinner gives the least indication of his desire to

return once more, then is his sweet Mother Mary ready to intercede for him and to bring him to the feet of Jesus.

Mary is the hope of the hopeless because she saves souls almost in spite of themselves and she brings them out of the clutches of the devils when they seem to be so ensnared that escape seems impossible. Oh, if we could only realize how Mary is the "Refuge of Sinners" and without her how many souls would be eternally lost. The saints in Heaven do very much for their friends on earth, but in the case of some souls, who have abused God's grace so much that hope of salvation seems practically impossible, what would be their fate if Mary would not come to their assistance? Her power of intercession is greater than all the saints put together, and she is continually engaged in snatching souls from the brink of Hell. This most sweet Mother seems to stand at the very gates of Hell to prevent souls from going into this abyss of torments. How many souls at the very last moment of life have turned to Mary when all hope seemed to be lost, and at the very last instant of life they were snatched from the fury of the devils. The very name of Mary strikes terror into the heart of the infernal abyss because the devils know that Mary robs them of more souls than all the saints in Heaven.

Devotion to Mary is what the devil and his agents hate most. When proud heretics rise up to destroy the Church of God, they seem bent upon heaping insults on this sweet Mother of Mercy, this Fountain of Hope, this consoler of the sorrowful. The statues of Mary in our churches or in our streets cause the enemies of the Church to foam with rage because these representations of this sweet Mother remind the faithful of her powers and her goodness. When we decorate her altars or keep her feastdays, the devil is enraged beyond all bounds, and on these occasions he stirs up his friends to heap some form of insult on her by showing public hatred or abuse to this Sweet Virgin. How many souls, by saying a single prayer to Mary before her statue or picture, have obtained some signal grace or favor which has made them henceforth lead lives which have eventually led to great heights of holiness. It is such a pity that the faithful will not have recourse to this sweet Mother of all graces.

Some struggle for a lifetime to overcome temptations and often fall into sin because they will not go to this sweet Mother and there lay all their cares in her maternal heart. She will obtain for them grace to overcome all their temptations, and she will carry them in her arms to the feet of Jesus. Some, after a life of sin, are anxious to return once more to Jesus, but fear their sinful habits might bring them back once more to the paths of error where their passions might be too strong for them. Oh, if these souls would only throw themselves at the feet of Mary, she would take them in her arms and protect them from all the terrors of the devils and all the fury of Hell. St. Gabriel of the Sorrowful Virgin was called by God to the religious life, but he again and again refused the invitation from the Sacred Heart of Jesus. On one occasion, when he was following a procession of Our Lady, the sweet Mother from her throne seemed to speak to him: "What are you doing in the world? Hasten to a monastery and become a religious." He shortly afterwards died a great saint. This sweet Mother had compassion on this youth who was refusing all the pleadings of the Sacred Heart, and she used her heavenly stratagems to make him accept the great graces which she was to obtain for him. How this saint must now thank Mary for her goodness in taking him in her arms as a mother would take her child! May this sweet Mother take each one who reads this in her arms and bestow upon them her choicest treasures.

Pompeo Batoni

MADONNA AND CHILD

OUR LADY OF MT. CARMEL

CHAPTER XIX

Our Lady of Mount Carmel

FOR two reasons, Mary is called Our Lady of Mount Carmel. The first is that Mary is the protector of the Carmelite Order throughout the world. She presented the Brown Scapular to St. Simon Stock as the pledge of her special protection over this order, promising that those who die wearing it would not suffer the pains of Hell. The second reason for the title of Our Lady of Mount Carmel is that Mary is the model of the interior life. The interior life is often confused with the hidden life. Some lead very hidden lives and never wish for public notice, and yet they are very far from being interior. Their lives may be external or exterior, and God may be very far from them.

The interior life means the life of union with God. Some people are engaged in active or external occupations and may be seen by all. Their external actions may be merely natural actions and may carry no supernatural reward. Even those engaged in the performance of works for the salvation of souls may gain very little merit from all their efforts, and their works may not bear very much supernatural fruit on account of the absence of the interior life of grace or the intimate union with God. Our Divine Lord spent only three years of His life in public, and even during these years He spent very much of His time in prayer. The sufferings and death on the Cross were really the chief end of the Incarnation. It was the interior sanctity of Jesus that gave the value to all His actions. We may compare the interior life with the branch and the vine. If the branch becomes withered, or if it ceases to draw the sap from the vine, it cannot bear fruit. In much the same way, unless we are united with Our Lord, our works will not be of value in the salvation of souls. This accounts for so many who have great mental qualities and great learning who are nonetheless useless in the works of salvation. They gain nothing for all their labors, and they make no use of all their knowledge, unless for the passing and empty applause or the lumber of the wealth of the world.

Now Mary is the model of the interior life because of the absence of anything extraordinary about her, as far as the eyes of the world could judge. Her works were only the common everyday duties performed by people of her state in life, and we see nothing striking in her actions. While Jesus was dying on Mount Calvary, Mary suffered with Jesus for the salvation of souls, and yet she was not noticed among the crowd. She may have had to suffer many insults on account of being the mother of one condemned as a criminal. She stood by the Cross and offered up all her ignominy and all her interior desolation and anguish for the salvation of souls. While Mary was at Nazareth, no one ever suspected the great dignity to which she was raised, and as far as the world was concerned, Mary was of no more consequence than anybody else. Yet she was the dearest to God of all His creatures, and she possessed privileges and graces unheard of before. She was the Mother of God, and this title gave her the right even to be obeyed by God Himself. What a subject for reflection, and how far short any honor we can pay to Mary will be to that which God Himself bestowed upon her! As any good son will obey his mother and as the parent has the right to obedience, honor and love from her child, so Mary can claim honor, love and obedience even from God. She had all these rights and privileges, and yet her life was not marked by any external signs of her unique powers. Only on one occasion did she use her position to bring about the working of a miracle, and this was to perform an act of charity and kindness. But even here no one is aware of the cause of the miracle. Mary does not even on this occasion give any external proof of her exalted dignity or holiness.

The interior life is little understood, even among those who do very much in many ways for the glory of God. The hidden and interior souls who are closely united to God are the chief instruments in the works of salvation. Others may do the supervision or may receive the credit or the praise, but those who are the foundation and the chief source of all the graces are generally hidden and unknown to the world. This is often the cause of great loss to souls because those called to work for souls do not appreciate the importance of the interior life, and so their works do not always last, nor do they themselves become nearer to God by all their exterior labors. The grass of the field dies off every year because its roots are near the surface, while the oak and the sycamore trees live for ages because their roots are deep. If we wish our works or our virtues to be lasting, we must go deep down into the interior life of grace and not merely be content with surface piety, which cannot stand the storms of trial and temptation.

In all the world there was no one so near to God as Mary was, and yet no one received so little of the world's applause. Even the friends of Jesus, with perhaps the exception of St. John, never realized the great holiness of her soul nor her importance in the work of Redemption. What then was the great secret of Mary's dignity and her unparalled holiness? This all sprang from her interior life. We can easily see why Carmel should be the special order of Mary, once we realize that the interior life means everything in the salvation of souls. The salvation of souls is brought about by the securing of God's grace. By the sufferings of Jesus the Church is filled with treasures for the salvation of all the souls in the world and for the relief of all the souls in Purgatory. The only problem is to bring these graces to our own souls and to the souls of others. Interior souls first sanctify themselves, and then they can be used to convey graces to others. The Communion of Saints means that the faithful on earth, the suffering in Purgatory, and the saints in Heaven can mutually assist each other. Interior souls in this world gain very many graces for the salvation of others, and in this way they also increase their own sanctity by their works of supernatural charity. The most charitable and the most meritorious of all works is to cooperate in the salvation of souls, and these interior souls obtain abundant graces for the conversion of sinners.

As Our Lord is the foundation of holiness and as the Blessed Sacrament is the source of all graces for souls, so Our Blessed Lady is our model in the work of sanctification. She did more for the salvation of souls than all the saints put together. She performed very few works that attracted attention, but her interior life gave to all her actions a value that surpassed any work performed by all the martyrs or all the confessors. All this arose from her interior holiness, or from the amount of grace in her soul. When Our Lady prayed at the Cross for the Good Thief, her prayer was heard, and when she prayed for the Jews and the soldiers, many of them were converted. Some may say that Mary was present on Calvary but that we have not that privilege. This is not quite true, because the Holy Sacrifice of the Mass is the renewal of the Sacrifice of Calvary, and we can pray at Mass with as much efficacy as if we were present at the Crucifixion of Jesus. Mary grew in grace every moment of her life because in the midst of her occupations she kept herself in the spirit of recollection by her purity of intention and because she offered each work for the love of God. It mattered not whether Mary nursed the Divine Infant or worked at Nazareth; she did everything to please God, and she sanctified her works by prayer and recollection. Even those who are not engaged in divine contemplations but who may have to perform exterior duties may sanctify themselves by the least good actions by offering each action to God for some good intention. Mary acted all through her life in conformity with God's will. When she was ordered to go into Egypt, she instantly obeyed, and thus she gained the merit of obedience as well as that of saving the life of Jesus. We see here how intelligent are those who cultivate the interior life. Mary had a beautiful intellect, and she was kindness itself to all who approached her. But she could realize that the performance of God's will must of necessity be the best for us because God loves us more than we love ourselves, and being all-wise and all-powerful, He knows what is good for us and can give us all graces and blessings. Mary therefore always acted in perfect conformity with God's will, and when God sent her crosses and trials, she made use of these to sanctify herself by offering her crosses for the salvation of souls. Those who, like Mary, cultivate the interior life are raised up to heights of holiness by their perfect conformity with God's will and by their patience under crosses and contradictions. These interior souls, like Our Lady, gain very many graces by their prayers and sacrifices for the salvation of others.

Towards the end of her life, Mary grew more and more in her union with God through her devotion to the Blessed Sacrament. She received Jesus every day in Holy Communion, and she spent most of her time in adoration before the Tabernacle, and this Heavenly Food and this long conversation with Jesus was the crowning of her interior life of sanctity. We must, like Mary, become interior if we wish to become holy or to be of use in the salvation of souls. The Blessed Sacrament is now the very food of this interior life. Our Lord said, "Unless you eat the flesh of the Son of Man and drink his blood, you shall not have life in you." The life here is the interior life of Sanctifying Grace. To become interior, we must be able to converse with Jesus in the Holy Eucharist. During our visits to the Prisoner of Love, and when Jesus visits us in Holy

Communion, we must be able to entertain Jesus, and we must be able to speak to Him and make known to Him all our wants and all our desires. The interior life can be perfected now by our love for Jesus in the Holy Eucharist. We must learn to talk to Jesus in our own words, and we must speak to Him with all the loving familiarity of a fond child addressing its Mother. Our words need not be measured. Jesus likes us to be free with Him. He will bestow upon us His sweet caress, and He will make known to us His secrets. He wishes us to pray much and offer to Him little sacrifices which He can apply to souls. Sinners will not take His favors. When we give Him our little sacrifices and our prayers for sinners, He can then so overpower them with grace that they can scarcely resist His pleadings. Oh, may Mary help us to understand the beauty and the value of the interior life!

C. Mariana

OUR LADY OF MT. CARMEL

OUR LADY OF THE ROSARY

CHAPTER XX

The Month of the Rosary

WE MAY judge of the excellence of the Rosary by the attention given to this devotion by the Vicar of Christ. The great Pope Leo XIII issued thirteen encyclicals on the Rosary and recommended this devotion as a family prayer for every Catholic home. The month of October has been specially selected as the "Month of the Rosary," and the feast of the Holy Rosary is now celebrated on the 7th of this month. This feast of the most Holy Rosary took its origin from the great victory of the Catholic forces over the Mohammedans at the battle of Lepanto on October 7th, 1571. The defeat of the enemies of the Church and of civilization was due to the special assistance of the Mother of God. The Rosary was recited throughout the countries of Europe for the success of the Christian forces, and the victory was attributed to Our Lady, called the "Help of Christians." The Rosary has been the great weapon against heresy and infidelity, but it is also the chief safeguard for family peace and holiness.

Our Holy Father wished to raise up the Rosary as a bulwark against the encroachments of the wicked and against the wiles of the devil aimed at the destruction of domestic sanctity. Society depends upon the family, and if we have good families, not all the powers of earth and Hell can make headway against the Church in her mission for the salvation of souls. We see some countries where the Faith has been preserved in spite of all the fury of Hell and in the face of all the powers of the world. How can we account for such steadfastness in the face of such trials? We must go deep down to the basis of social virtue to get the explanation of such heroism, and when we go deep enough, we will find family holiness in these countries. If we examine a little more, we will find that the chief means of preserving this sanctity in family life was the practice of the Rosary as a family prayer.

The great St. Dominic performed a wonderful work in the destruction of the Albigensian heresy. He had spent a long time in arguments with the heretics, and as is usual he made no converts by his arguments. Never has there yet been a single conversion made by arguments or dispute alone because heretics, as a rule, do not wish to know the Truth. The devil knows all the truths of the Church even better than many Catholics, and yet he has no wish to serve God. While Our Lord was dying on the Cross, He prayed for his executioners, and He excused them on the grounds that they knew not what they did. Our Lord's prayer was heard and thousands were converted through this act of forgiveness who would never have received such a grace had not the suffering and merciful Heart of Jesus prayed for them. Jesus here excuses them on account of ignorance, but in the case of many of these people, their ignorance was culpable. They could have known the truth if they had wished, but they resembled the coward, Pilate, who asked, "What is truth?" but did not wait for an answer. Arguing over religious matters with those outside the Church only gives the enemies of God an opportunity to blaspheme and to mock at holy things. Reason unaided by grace is not able to grasp the great religious truths contained in the Catholic Church.

It may be asked then what are we to do with a view to instructing those outside the Faith? We must, like St. Dominic, teach the simple Christian doctrine and we may answer the objections of and give information to those who are sincerely anxious to know the Truth. The Church spread throughout the great pagan Roman empire by the preaching of the Gospel, aided by the blood of the martyrs and the prayers of the faithful. When a nation or an individual loses the Faith, it is never for intellectual reasons nor because they cannot harmonize the beliefs of the Church with their philosophy of life. The Faith is lost through the loss of grace owing to absence of prayer and through the commission of sin. The Faith in a country is preserved by the teaching of Christian doctrine and by the self-sacrificing lives of the faithful. Sanctity is only self-denial for the love of God. Some perform self-sacrificing actions, but for some worldly motive, and so that is not sanctity. The marks of true sanctity are prayer, self-denial and zeal for God's glory.

When St. Dominic found that his arguments were of no value, he had recourse to the Mother of God, who has always been the consoler of the afflicted and the help of all those who carry on works for the salvation of souls. This sweet Mother told the saint to lay aside the arguments and begin the teaching of the simple Christian doctrine. The message of the angel to Mary was the beginning of the work of Redemption, and St. Dominic taught the people to repeat this Angelic Salutation, which at once reminded them of the great mystery of the Incarnation. St. Dominic at once gave up his arguments with the heretics and began to teach the people to pray to Mary by repeating the Hail Mary. While he repeated the Our Fathers and the Hail Marys, he taught the people in simple language some mystery of Our Lord's life. In a short time the people gave up their heresy and returned once more to the practice of their religion. We see here the importance of prayer in the work of salvation. Prayer removes the obstacles to the reception of grace, and simple instruction will do the rest. Prayer obtains everything from God, simply because one who prays prepares his soul for the seeds of grace and sanctification, and if only heretics and all those outside the Church could be induced to pray, they would very soon receive the gift of the Faith. The absence of prayers means the absence of grace, and so the evils of sin and heresy are all due in the final result to the want of prayer.

We must not leave out another factor in the destruction of the Albigensian heresy, and that was the power of the intercession of Mary. St. Dominic prayed to Our Lady, and he taught the people to do so. Mary is the link that binds the soul to Jesus. She is also the link that binds whole nations to Jesus, and so we have another explanation of the marvelous success of St. Dominic. Those who invoke the aid of this Holy Mother are assured of success because her prayers are so powerful that they can defeat all the powers of Hell and all the stratagems of wicked men. It is worthy of notice also that the Order of St. Dominic remained so faithful to the Church during the time of the Reformation. This is accounted for by their devotion to the Rosary and by their fidelity to the teaching of the ordinary Christian doctrine to the faithful. St. Thomas, who was perhaps after St. Dominic the greatest gem of the Dominican order, so simplified the philosophy and the theology of the Church that when the time of trial came, the sons of St. Dominic were ready to give a simple explanation of all the truths of the Church, and in this way they were able to confound all the tricks of the heretics.

The Rosary has been the great safeguard of whole nations during times of storm and stress when the wolves of heresy threatened to devour the faithful children of Jesus and Mary. When priests were put to death, it was practically impossible to preserve the Faith for the want of assistance of the Sacraments and on account of the absence of religious instruction. The devotion to the Rosary kept the Faith in whole countries, and we have no reason to be surprised at this. The simple meditations of the Rosary on the lives of Jesus and Mary and the consideration of some mystery of faith kept the knowledge of the supernatural truths before the minds of the faithful, and the prayers or the repetition of the Our Father and Hail Mary reminded the people of the Angelical Salutation and the Providence of God, while it at the same time prepared the soul for and obtained grace by the power of impetration, or by its efficacy as a prayer. This devotion of the Rosary has been the great secret of family holiness and has therefore been the source of vocations and of much of the sanctity of the Church. Vocation can only spring from good families, and saints always come from homes in which Jesus and Mary have a prominent place and in which the family is sanctified each evening by the recitation of the Rosary, which draws down the blessings and the protection of this sweet Mother.

We mean by goodness in families, supernatural goodness. Many families may be respectable and may enjoy the goodwill of their neighbors, but their goodness may be purely or largely natural, and may take no account of eternity. Some are here confused and they may tend to copy the natural goodness of others because they cannot distinguish between the natural and the supernatural. Some ask why do worldlings prosper, while the good have to suffer. This is again confusing the natural and the supernatural. Worldlings, or those who act as if this world were the only world, may prosper and be respected in this world, and God gives them this reward for their natural good works. But there is no word here of the supernatural rewards of eternity, which surpass any of the passing joys of this world. Our Lord never promised worldly rewards to His followers. The friends of Jesus may receive the gifts of this world, but these are only accidental. Our Lord advised His friends to lay up "treasures in Heaven" where they cannot be destroyed and where thieves do not steal. The hundredfold promised even in this life may not necessarily consist of wealth or honors. It may and generally does consist of blessings, which bring true peace of soul and prevent many misfortunes. But the supernatural reward promised to those who seek first the Kingdom of God will begin on the shores of eternity and will be never-ending. The family Rosary will prevent those unhappy occurrences in the home which cause such sadness for both parents and children and which often end in the destruction of the matrimonial bond. The family Rosary is one of the best prayers of the Church. Prayer is intended to raise the mind to God and to take our thoughts away from the passing affairs of this world. The Rosary is long enough to engage our attention for a sufficient time to enable us to leave aside our worldly cares, and this is good for both body and soul. It can be said on a journey or even when engaged in our occupations which do not demand all our attention. The indulgences of the Rosary are so great that the faithful ought to make use of this devotion for the relief of the souls in Purgatory. The Rosary is the devotion which belongs especially to Our Lady. No one who wishes for the assistance of Mary will neglect her Rosary.

Sassoferrato

QUEEN OF THE MOST HOLY ROSARY

OUR LADY OF LA SALETTE

CHAPTER XXI

Our Lady of La Salette

ON SATURDAY, the 19th of September 1846, two peasant children were guarding their master's cattle near the mountain of La Salette, near Grenoble in France. About midday a beautiful lady appeared to the children who, by her conversation and appearance, was afterwards recognized to be the Blessed Virgin. Our Lady appeared sorrowful and spoke to the children about the punishment which was about to fall on the people on account of their irreligious lives. Our Lady spoke of two sins in particular which were causing sorrow to her Divine Son. The first was the neglect of the sanctification of Sunday. The second was the improper use made of the Name of God. When public calamities fall upon a people, many causes are assigned for their occurrence, but the fundamental cause is the irreligion of the people.

When people act as if this world were the only world and when they make no provision for eternity, it is then that Our Lord in His mercy sends them temporal calamities in order to take their hearts from the inordinate love of wealth and luxury. When people are blessed with abundance of the goods of this world, they as a general rule have no desire for heavenly things, and they make their paradise of this earth with its empty pleasures and unstable wealth. It might be expected, if people had deep faith, that they would give thanks to God for His blessings instead of using these very gifts of God to offend Him and to set their hearts upon them, instead of giving their hearts to God. Avarice is a species of idolatry. The pagans worshipped idols as symbols of nature's gifts and as an excuse to gratify their passions. Worldlings, or those who think only of this world, give their hearts and their thoughts to the things of this world, although they do not now as a rule use any sign or offer incense to a piece of wood as did the pagans of old—when they wished to preserve their worldly customs and keep up the paganism upon which society was then based. In some secret societies and in some Masonic gatherings, there is still carried on this worship of nature under some symbol.

This is only a part of paganism towards which certain elements in society are constantly tending in their efforts to destroy the Catholic Church. But when we place such importance on any earthly thing or anything which is intended merely for the temporal welfare of man as to make it the end of existence, then we are only going back to paganism. The cry of Our Lord in this world, which has been taken up by all the followers of Jesus, is, "Lay not up treasures on earth, where moth and rust both corrupt and thieves break through and steal, but lay up for yourselves treasures in heaven where thieves do not break through and steal." Those who give their hearts to worldly wealth or to the gaining of worldly glory are doing the very opposite of what Our Lord commanded His followers to do. Paganism was also an excuse for the worship of the state, which is only another way of giving our whole hearts to the things of this world. In the same way, those who now put the state before the Church or who think only of the welfare of the state are putting this world before God. They are giving the honor due to God to some creature, which is only a species of idolatry. It is so very easy and it is so very common, even among those who are looked upon as religious, to give too much attention to worldly things and to the amassing of wealth or to the desire for self-gratification.

The apparition of Our Lady at La Salette has been instrumental in preventing many punishments from falling upon the people—by her warning of the cause of most of the calamities that befall nations and countries. Our Lady first complained of the refusal of the people to give at least one day of the week to the service of

God. So many wrong views exist about the sanctification of Sunday that it may be well to give a few words on the meaning of this day of rest. This day of each week is intended to recreate both body and mind and to give leisure to attend to the welfare of the soul. The abstaining from servile works and the attendance at Mass are laid down by the Church as just the minimum to be done in order to avoid sin. But the chief end of this day is to give leisure to attend to the eternal things. This does not mean that the rest of the week is to be given over entirely to the affairs of this world. All our works are to be sanctified by daily prayer and by offering all our labors in the spirit of penance for our sanctification. By this means we gain grace by all our actions, if we perform them for the love of God and if by prayer and by frequenting the Sacraments we preserve the state of Sanctifying Grace in our souls.

But this one day each week is ordained by God as a day which belongs specially to God, and on this day we are expected to promote especially the work of our sanctification. It reminds us of the eternal rest of Paradise after our few years of struggle in this world. The great secret of spending Sunday properly does not consist in providing amusements for the people to keep them occupied or to discuss ways and means of keeping them from sin on that day. It is terrible to think that so many sins are committed on the one day which ought to be devoted to our sanctification. The whole matter is to educate the people to a proper understanding of the object of the Sunday rest. The day is not intended to be spent solely either in idleness or in sport and amusement. On this day each week, our time ought to be devoted to the performance of those works which, directly and indirectly, tend to our sanctification. Besides attending Mass, the faithful ought to nourish their souls on this day with the Heavenly Food of Holy Communion. It is time that the faithful realized the necessity of being spiritually nourished, and they ought to know that the cause of practically all the sins committed in Catholic countries is the want of an appreciation of the value and the necessity of Holy Communion for leading holy lives. People may lead naturally good lives without this Heavenly Food, but for the performance of supernatural good actions and for the preservation of the supernatural life of the soul, we require the supernatural nourishment of the Body and Blood of Jesus in Holy Communion. The knights and handmaids of the Blessed Sacrament will do much for the sanctification of the world by encouraging frequent Communion. Besides Mass and Holy Communion, it would be a beautiful custom to spend part of Sunday in visiting Our Lord in the Blessed Eucharist. These weekly visits to Jesus would keep people away from evil company, and by their loving converse with Jesus they would gain light and grace to avoid the dangers which beset so many souls on their journey to Heaven. Good reading is another way to spend the leisure time of the Sunday, and this will be an easy way to keep up the knowledge of the Christian doctrine, which all are bound to acquire and to preserve. Catholic books, papers and magazines are now so numerous that there is no excuse for people to spend their time in reading worldly newspapers and dangerous novels.

At La Salette Our Lady complained to the children of the improper use of the Holy Name of Jesus. It is such a pity to hear people using the Name of Jesus with irreverence and bringing it into every subject of dispute or conversation, as if this were only a name to be treated with contempt. The contempt shown to this Name means disrespect to Our Lord, and this Name was made known by the Angel Gabriel as the special name chosen by God for the Redeemer of the world. Reverence for the Name of Jesus ought to be the mark of all those who love Jesus, and it ought to be the special sign of the friends of Our Lord or of those who are members of the True Church.

Our Lady also asked the children if they said their prayers well. She recommended them to be diligent in saying their morning and night prayers and, if in the morning they had no time for more, they ought at least to say the Our Father and the Hail Mary. It will only be at the Judgment Day that people will know the value of the few minutes given to morning and evening prayers. When people cannot attend Mass and receive Holy Communion each morning, then the only supernatural food for their souls is prayer. Morning and evening prayer is just as necessary for the preservation of the supernatural life as food and air are to preserve our natural life. The life of Sanctifying Grace, which is the supernatural life of the soul, requires care and attention, just like the body. The body requires food, air and clothing, and the mind requires the mental food of knowledge. The soul requires the supernatural food of Holy Communion, plus prayer and self-denial, while the mind requires the supernatural food of Christian doctrine. Without morning and evening prayer it is practically impossible to preserve the life of Sanctifying Grace, and as the body requires frequent feeding, so must the soul have God's grace, which is secured by prayer. Absence of morning and evening prayer means that the soul has not strength to overcome temptations, nor will it have any zeal for spiritual things. It will have no zeal to grow in holiness, and it will not be able to appreciate heavenly truths.

We see in the apparition of La Salette the goodness and sweetness of Mary. She was so anxious for the welfare of the world that she wished to avert the calamities threatened on account of the sins of the people. This sweet Mother pleads for us with all the tenderness of a mother's love, and oh, what a number of misfortunes are prevented by her kindness and her pleading prayers! How often does she stay the hand of God when it is raised to strike a sinful and ungrateful people. Can we ever thank Our Lady enough for all her interest in us and for all her efforts for the salvation of souls—poor souls, who will not accept the gifts of Jesus and who will make no efforts to save themselves! Mary pleads for them, and she uses the sweet ingenuity of her beautiful mind to find ways and means to prevent calamities and to bring the people to the everlasting rewards of Paradise. How the sweet and Immaculate Heart of Mary loves us! How carefully she watches over her children! Mary wishes us to sanctify ourselves, and then she wishes her dear children to help by their prayers and good example in the salvation of souls. Increase in devotion to Mary will mean the salvation of whole countries. No child of Mary will be allowed to perish. This sweet Mother has never yet lost one of her children.

OUR LADY OF LA SALETTE

Murillo

THE IMMACULATE CONCEPTION

CHAPTER XXII

The Blue Scapular
of the Immaculate Conception

WE will never be able to thank God sufficiently for making us members of the one and only True Church. Those unfortunate souls who are cut off from the Church by infidelity, heresy or schism are indeed to be pitied because they are living in spiritual starvation and they cannot make use of the spiritual food which the Church alone can give, because they are outside her fold and have not the supernatural life of Sanctifying Grace. Our Lord's Passion and Death has filled the Church with treasures in such abundance, that once we have the good fortune to become members of the Church of God, we have no need for any more anxiety about our eternal salvation. Once we have secured the state of grace, or once we have received the supernatural birth of Sanctifying Grace, we have no further reason to fear for eternity.

This state of grace is secured by Baptism, and if one has the great misfortune of losing this grace by the commission of sin, we have the Sacrament of Penance by which we are again restored to God's friendship and to the supernatural life of sanctification. It is very easy to preserve and increase the state of grace in our souls by performing supernatural good works. We can perform these with ease by securing God's assistance, which can be obtained by prayer and by feeding our souls with Holy Communion. We have only to secure all possible graces if we wish to become saints. The truly wise man endeavors to secure grace, while the fool sets his heart on the empty things of this world.

The whole trouble with the children of our Holy Mother the Church is their want of appreciation of the value of

all these treasures and graces. How very easy it is for
a member of the True Church to reach not only salvation, but a very high degree of holiness! How very easy
it is for a Catholic to pass from this world without even
passing through Purgatory! We have every grace and
every assistance we can wish for, and it only remains for
us to make use of all the treasures which are at our disposal. If a man were hungry because he would not eat
food, then if he dies of starvation he has only himself
to blame, for no one can compel him to take food. In
the same way, if a soul is spiritually starved in the midst
of heavenly treasures, then if such a soul is lost, she can
only blame herself for her misfortune. What pains the
Heart of Jesus, in the case of those who are members
of His Church, is their want of appreciation of all He has
done for them and their refusal to accept His blessings.
Prayer will obtain any grace asked for, and yet so few
will even ask for graces. Holy Communion will nourish
the soul and enable it to grow in grace and give it a rel-
ish for spiritual things, and yet this great treasure, this
fountain of holiness, is not sufficiently made use of.

Many souls are in Purgatory and are suffering very
much for their faults simply because no one will pray
or make any sacrifice for them. The Church is filled with
graces, and she has opened her treasures to the faithful
for the remission even of the temporal punishment due
to sin by the means of indulgences. In this way she gives
the faithful an opportunity of satisfying for their past
sins in this world, and at the same time she gives them
the opportunity of growing in grace and of assisting the
Poor Souls in Purgatory. The Stations of the Cross are
so richly indulgenced that the making of the Way of the
Cross will be very efficacious for the relief of the souls
in Purgatory, and at the same time this devotion will beget
within our hearts true love of Our Lord and heartfelt sorrow for our sins. What a pity that this devotion is not
made more use of for the conversion of sinners and for

the relief of the suffering souls. It would at the same time sanctify all those who practiced it.

The devotion to the Blue Scapular of the Immaculate Conception is enriched with so many graces and indulgences that it is such a pity that so few even know of this treasure of graces. Like the Scapular of Our Lady of Mount Carmel, the little Blue Scapular is a representation of the large blue habit worn by the Theatine congregation of religious. Like the Brown Scapular, which was given by Our Lady as a sign of her protection for the Order of Mount Carmel, so the Blue Scapular is a sign of the protection of Mary for the Theatines, who are specially devoted to the Immaculate Conception. The little Blue Scapular of the Immaculate Conception is worn to honor Our Lady under this title. The chief virtue which ought to characterize those who wear the livery of this Immaculate Mother is heavenly purity, and their chief occupation ought to be to promote, by all means, good morals by their good example and by their prayers for the conversion of sinners.

The most striking aspects of the devotion to the Blue Scapular are the numerous graces and indulgences attached to the wearing of it. The indulgences are beyond all calculation. The only conditions are that one be properly invested in the Scapular by a priest who has the faculties to invest, that the person be in the state of grace, and that he or she say six times the Our Father, the Hail Mary and the Glory Be to the Father. These six Our Fathers, six Hail Marys and six Glory Be to the Fathers can be said as many times in the day as we wish, and each time we say this prayer while wearing this Blue Scapular, we gain all the indulgences of the seven principal churches in Rome, of the churches of the Portiuncula of Jerusalem, and of St. James of Compostella in Spain. These prayers are to be offered in honor of the Blessed Trinity and of Mary conceived without sin and for all the intentions of Our Holy Father the Pope. These intentions are the exaltation of the Catholic Church, the extermination of heresies and concord among Christian peoples, and the welfare of the Holy See.

Here is a veritable mine of spiritual treasures, and yet so few make proper use of all these privileges. If we would but make use of these treasures of graces, we would soon empty Purgatory, and we would gain great heights of sanctity by our meritorious actions and our supernatural charity. Some seem to think, when they offer their prayers for sinners and their indulgences for the souls in Purgatory, that they will lose by doing so. This is well worthy of deep consideration, and it will be well to have correct views on all these matters. It is a good work to feed the hungry or to clothe the naked, but it is much more meritorious to save our neighbor's soul, and we will gain a much greater reward from the salvation of even one soul than from the feeding of all the hungry in the world or from making everyone in this world rich in worldly goods.

If by our prayers and penances we help in the spread of the Faith or in the conversion of sinners, we increase the state of Sanctifying Grace in our souls, and so we increase our glory for eternity. In the application of indulgences to the souls in Purgatory, we gain the merit of a great act of supernatural charity, every time we help to alleviate or to shorten the sufferings of one of these poor souls. Devotion to the souls in Purgatory is therefore a fruitful means of holiness and an easy way to secure blessings from God. Those who wear the Blue Scapular could gain these numerous indulgences many times each day without very much inconvenience. These prayers could be said as we are going on the tram or train or while walking or working, and they can be said in about two minutes. Just reflect on the good that can be accomplished by spending two minutes in reciting the six Our Fathers, Hail Marys and Glory Be to the Fathers. How many souls in Purgatory can we release and how much good we can do for the welfare of the Church and of souls!

The Blue Scapular reminds us also that we are the children of this Immaculate Mother, and therefore we must imitate her virtues. The virtue of purity is the specially beloved virtue of Mary, and those who are her children will take all the means available to preserve this jewel of the soul. Purity is preserved principally by prayer, and those who fail in this angelic virtue owe their fall to the want of prayer. The three Hail Marys said morning and night in the honor of the Immaculate Conception of Mary will work wonders in the preservation of purity. Many a life of sin has been avoided by the faithful practice of these three Hail Marys. Perhaps there is no title of Our Lady so efficacious for obtaining graces as that of her Immaculate Conception. It is such a pity that the faithful do not ask Mary for favors and pray to her in honor of this great privilege of her Immaculate Conception, which was the foundation of all her other privileges and graces.

The consecration of the purity of their souls by many a boy or girl to this sweet Mother Immaculate has been the means of preserving countless souls from sin and has in many cases ended in their being called to the religious life, which has eventuated in their gaining great holiness. Why will not all the faithful become children of Mary? If only one particle of the goodness and power of Mary were known, sin would soon cease to exist among Mary's children, and millions would rush to the arms of Mary, and there they would be safe forever. It is so easy to become one of Our Lady's children. We have merely to ask this sweet Mother to accept us and to look upon us as her children. Her devotions are so easy and so powerful that, by following them, we gain countless graces and are assured of her protection. It is easy to wear her Scapular, to keep her feasts—by receiving the Body and Blood of Jesus on those days—and to say her Rosary every day with the three additional Hail Marys night and morning. We have only to go to the feet of this Mother and as little children ask her to take us and to watch over us. She will embrace us with all the tenderness of a mother who sets her eyes on her child after a long absence. How Mary loves her children, and how she caresses them and smiles upon them! At the last moments of their lives, Mary comes to them and all the devils fly at her approach. She watches over her children at the critical moments of their lives, but at the last moment, Mary will not fail them. A child of Mary has nothing to fear in life or death. She will ask her Son to receive her children with open arms, and Mary will be refused nothing by Jesus. Oh, may this sweet Mother be the consoler of the dying, and may all the children of Mary prove themselves worthy of such a privilege of being the chosen sons and daughters of this tender Mother. If sinners could be induced to say the three Hail Marys in honor of her Immaculate Conception, their sinful lives would soon cease. If those outside the Church could be induced to pray to Mary, they would soon be received within the fold of God's Church. O Mary, conceived without sin, pray for us who have recourse to thee.

> Do we ever think of a day that is coming,
>   A terrible day when we shall cry
> For one little prayer to ease our anguish,
>   To soften the anger of God on high?
>
> We know not when—it may be tomorrow—
>   When all the world is fair and bright:
> Have pity upon them; have pity upon them.
>   Pray for the suffering souls tonight.

THE IMMACULATE CONCEPTION

MOTHER OF GOOD COUNSEL

CHAPTER XXIII

Our Lady of Good Counsel

THE HOLY Ghost through the mouth of the "Wise Man" advises us to take counsel in all important matters, but He is careful to state that we ought to take advice only from those who have true knowledge and true wisdom or prudence. It is useless and even pernicious to follow the advice of foolish people, but it shows also great absence of prudence to follow our own opinion in the face of the advice of many who are qualified by their position and their training to direct others. The Psalmist says, "I have had more learning than those who taught me because thy testimonies have been my meditation." Again the Psalmist says, "I have had learning above my elders because I have sought after thy commandments." We see here that old age and great knowledge are not the only requisites for guidance, for the Royal Prophet in his youth had more knowledge than his elders because he endeavored to understand heavenly things.

A person may be young and inexperienced in worldly matters, and yet he may have plenty of knowledge through the inspirations of the Holy Ghost because of his holiness of life. We must also distinguish between worldly knowledge and heavenly knowledge. One may be learned and prudent in all worldly matters and may understand very much about the money markets of the world and may even know much about philosophy and literature. Yet in heavenly things, such a one may be a very bad guide. For the Christian, and more especially for those who are members of the True Church, it is good to take advice from those who are well versed in heavenly things. Although we are aiming at and preparing for Heaven, yet we must live in this world, and by our good conduct and by supernaturalizing all our actions we must gain the everlasting crown of glory.

We see in Our Lord's life how, with all His sweetness and straightforwardness, He was able to thwart all the designs of His enemies until He wished to lay down His life for us, and then He made use of their malice to redeem the world by His death on the Cross. When He was asked a question that He did not wish to answer, He replied to His enemies by asking them another question. When He was asked about the End of the World, He replied in such a way that He left the Apostles in doubt about the time so that they might always be prepared. The early Christians kept many of their secrets from the pagans so that they might escape persecution and so that they might be able to carry out their religious obligations in the catacombs underneath the very city of Rome itself.

We see this quality of counsel or prudence in those saints who were raised up by God for special purposes. St. Joan of Arc was able to confound all her enemies, and she was able to baffle them in all their diabolical designs upon her. She had the gift of counsel and her fervent prayers kept her near to God, and so she was enlightened by the Holy Ghost. When the saintly Cure of Ars was being persecuted by his enemies, he was able to baffle all their designs upon him. These holy souls were so enlightened by the Holy Ghost that they were able to defeat all the snares of their enemies and all the wiles of the devil.

In all the events of life it is useful to have the gift of counsel or heavenly prudence. This will prevent us from making many mistakes and so will enable us to do much more for God and for our own sanctification. In the world there are plenty of generous souls who could do very much for God's glory if they had only the gifts of the Holy Ghost. They simply do not know what to do, or they cannot do the correct thing. They may do good deeds but at the wrong time and in the wrong circumstances; or they may do good, but still they could do very much better if only they had this beautiful gift of counsel. Their want of counsel generally arises from neglect of prayer. They never pray for counsel or understanding; and so they make mistake after mistake, and instead of sanctifying themselves, they generally waste most of their lives on unimportant trifles and in useless worries. It is such a pity to see people wasting their health and their time in worrying over the mistakes of life because, if we wish to worry over things, we could spend all our valuable time doing so, and in the end we will be no better off.

This world is an imperfect world at its best, and we can only make the best of what we have, but these imperfections and troubles are intended to sanctify us by training us to meekness, patience, prayer, and fortitude, and in this way we will gain the everlasting reward of Paradise. But even in the imperfections of this world, we will find that some can come through without much mishap and without much anxiety. They seem to be able to get all they want. What is the secret of their happiness and their success at gaining God's grace? They merely are friendly with the Holy Ghost, and their minds are so enlightened that they can do great things and gain much grace without very much trouble. The great secret of the whole matter is prayer. If we pray, we will obtain all we ask. When some want any favor, they gain indulgences and offer Masses and Holy Communions for the souls in Purgatory, and this act of supernatural charity gains for them many spiritual and temporal blessings. Some are anxious for spiritual blessings for themselves or their children, and they pray and offer Masses and Holy Communions for the conversion of sinners, and this greatest act of supernatural charity obtains for themselves wonderful blessings and draws down graces upon all their friends or those who are dear to them.

Our Blessed Lady has very many titles which remind us of her power on behalf of her clients and her children. The title of ''Our Lady of Good Counsel'' is one that has never yet been fully appreciated, and yet counsel or good advice is the very thing that most people need, and it is useful in every event in life. In Our Lady's life we notice how she was guided by the gift of counsel, or heavenly prudence. She was so prudent that for thirty years she never divulged the secret of the Incarnation. She was so prudent that she baffled the cunning of Herod who sought to destroy Jesus, and she took the Divine Infant into Egypt. She never appeared during the three years of Our Lord's Public Life because Jesus wished then to prove His divinity, and so the time for giving public honor to His Mother had not yet arrived. She knew how to wait for God's good time.

It is a source of many mistakes to be in too great a hurry to perform good works, and on the other hand, some allow God's grace to pass by without profiting by it. Many vocations are lost through delay, and many good works are spoiled by undue hurry. Many young people attempt what is beyond their grace, and many do not go about matters in the right way. All these mistakes cause great loss to souls and prevent people from becoming holy. Others are merely the tools of the devil, who endeavors to prevent good works by making souls scrupulous when he cannot succeed in any other way. The way of childlike simplicity or perfect trust in the goodness of the Sacred Heart of Jesus is the outcome of this gift of counsel. The Little Flower of Jesus certainly had this heavenly gift, as we see by her confidence and abandonment to Jesus. She could make no mistake in trusting to Jesus, and she was wise enough to know that all Our Lord wanted was our good and our happiness. Our Lord says, "My child, give me thy heart," and this Servant of God gave her heart to the sweet Jesus, and she cast all her cares and all faults into the flames of love with which this sweet Heart burns for souls.

The gift of counsel is necessary, especially in youth, but it is useful all through life. It is useful and necessary to those who may have charge of others or who may have to direct others. It is necessary if we are to avoid the snares of the devil. Many young people are caught in the snares of wickedness who, if they had proper advice, would do very much for God. What a pity that the source of Good Counsel, the Mother of Jesus, is so much neglected! Mary had to direct the infantile and boyish steps of the God-Man. The Saviour of the world obeyed and followed the directions of Mary for thirty years. Surely she must have had the gift of counsel to direct God Himself for so many years. The powers of Mary are far beyond our understanding. Mary had the right to command God Himself. God Himself obeyed Mary during His life on earth, and He obeys her still in His Kingdom of glory.

If Mary can direct God Himself, surely she can advise or counsel her children in this vale of tears. Her maternal heart found a way out of the difficulty at the marriage feast at Cana, and she will find a way out of every difficulty for us if only we will have recourse to her. Some may object that they do not know when she speaks to them. Mary is very easily approached. She will listen to all our requests. If we are in doubt or if we do not know what direction to take, let us ask Mary to help us. If we will only offer up the Rosary a few times, we will find our minds quite clear—even in very difficult situations. When we have any very important decision to make, it is not good to act in haste or without prayer. If we will wait a little and pray, our minds will be enlightened and our paths will be made clear. If we cannot attend Mass or receive Holy Communion, we can surely offer the Rosary for a few times, and we will be preserved from all dangers and be preserved from making mistakes. In the events of everyday life, we could so easily say a few Hail Marys to Our Lady of Good Counsel to guide us in all our actions. When we are in little trials or difficulties, we could very easily keep praying to Our Lady and asking her assistance, and we would be sure to do what was right and what would be for our present and future good. Sometimes we are too anxious for a certain course of action, and we may think that everything is clear. Perhaps we do not see far enough. The present good may be only a snare of the devil for our destruction. It is here where prayer to Mary is so useful. It is better never to act without asking counsel in prayer, and if matters seem very clear to us, it may be all the more necessary to wait and pray. Our Lady will not allow the devil to deceive us if we ask her counsel and if we follow her directions, which will come to our minds in prayer.

> O Virgin Mother, Lady of Good Counsel,
>   Sweetest picture artist ever drew,
> In all my doubts I fly to thee for guidance;
>   Mother, tell me, what am I to do?
>
> Life, alas, is often dark and dreary!
>   Cheating shadows hide the truth from view.
> When my soul is most perplexed and weary,
>   Mother, tell me, what am I to do?

MOTHER OF GOOD COUNSEL

IMMACULATE HEART OF MARY

CHAPTER XXIV

The Immaculate Heart of Mary

THE devotion to the Sacred Heart of Jesus has at last become worldwide, and we have every reason to rejoice for the future of the Church on this account. This devotion to the Heart of Jesus will mean the reign of this Sacred Heart throughout the world, and in good time Jesus will draw all the nations to Himself by means of the allurements and the affections of His Divine Heart. Side by side with the devotion to the Heart of Jesus we may rank the devotion to the sweet Heart of Mary. The Heart of Jesus came from Mary, and the sweetness and tenderness of this Adorable Heart of Jesus is largely due to the purity and generosity of the Heart of His Holy Mother. We are very liable to forget that Jesus owes much of the beauty of His Personality to the sweetness and kindness of Mary. We all owe much to our mothers, and Jesus is no exception.

We honor the heart of Mary above all the members of her immaculate body on account of her sweetness and her nobility of character. As the Heart of Jesus represents to us all the love of Our Lord for us, so does the Immaculate Heart of Mary manifest to us her love for us, for whom her Divine Son suffered so much. The chief characteristic of Our Lady is her sweetness and kindness. She watches over her children with all the tenderness of a mother, and she obtains from Jesus abundant graces for all those who approach her. We often see great religious orders started in the Church which are largely instrumental in the preservation and the diffusion of the Faith and therefore in the salvation of countless souls. But we will always notice that Mary has had a share in all these foundations and that the chief instruments in every work for the salvation of others were merely acting under the guidance and protection of the Mother of God. Mary gave Jesus to the world, and she now distributes the special graces gained by the sufferings of her Divine Son throughout the various nations of the earth. Mary gave her consent to be the Mother of Jesus. She offered Him in the Temple, and she consummated her offering on Calvary. Without Mary we would not have had Jesus, and so Mary has now the right to distribute the graces gained by Jesus by His death on the Cross.

It is really a cause of terrible loss to souls that the sweetness of Mary is not more dwelt upon nor the power of her intercession sufficiently appreciated. Very many earnest souls struggle a long time to reach holiness and to overcome their faults. If they would have recourse to Mary, they would be taught the way of true sanctity, and their difficulties would soon vanish. The whole secret of the success of Our Lady is the power of her prayers. The efficacy of the prayers of a saint depends exactly on the amount of grace in the soul. Even during life the prayers of a holy person are very powerful and are in proportion to the holiness he has reached. After death the powers of intercession of a saint are neither cancelled nor diminished. But in the case of Mary, the measure of the success of her intercession corresponds with her position in Heaven. Mary had more grace in her soul at the first moment of her Immaculate Conception than any saint has ever reached, even after a life spent in the service of God. But if Mary was so pure and so holy at her Immaculate Conception, what must not her holiness have been at the moment of her death? No child of Adam ever suffered so much as Mary, and no one ever acted in all her sufferings with such conformity with God's will. The power of her intercession now surpasses that of all the saints combined, and so we can form some idea of her influence in the salvation of souls. Her Rosary has destroyed many heresies in the Church and has kept the Faith in many countries and has brought blessings to

countless families. The three Hail Marys said morning and
evening in honor of her Immaculate Conception have kept
millions of souls in the virtue of purity and have thereby
sown the seeds of countless vocations to the religious life.
Her statues have reminded many of her virtues and have
induced numbers to pray to her, with the result that they
received from her the choicest graces. No one can have
a tender love for Mary and not have a love for Jesus.
Mary brings her children to Jesus and entices them to
nourish themselves with His Body and Blood.

The sweetness of the Immaculate Heart of Mary gives
her no rest, day or night. She is constantly engaged in
assisting her children and guarding them from all dangers.
Oh, when will souls ever learn to appreciate the goodness and tenderness of this sweet Mother? She is wait-
ing to give us her blessings and to protect us from all
the snares of the devil, but so few will accept her gifts
or become her children. Mary cannot give her gifts to
those who will not receive them. How many pass by
graces or refuse them, with the result that countless souls
are lost. Every grace accepted means the increase of grace
in others. Every soul sanctified means the sanctification
of countless other souls. One saint will give more glory
to God and be the means of saving more souls than thousands of others who are content with mediocrity. Oh, how
Mary desires to raise up saints in the Church, but so few
will approach her or accept her protection and her powerful intercession. A single prayer from Mary opens the
treasures of Heaven and obtains extraordinary graces for
any soul that is willing or ready to accept them. What
the Church needs most in all ages and in all countries
is saints. A saint is merely a channel for conveying graces
to souls, and when a saint is found in the priesthood,
his power of saving souls is little short of that of Jesus
Himself. Jesus has given all power to His priests, and the
great desire of both Jesus and Mary is the sanctification
of the priesthood. Next to the priesthood, Mary wishes

to raise up saints in every walk of life, but especially in parents and in mothers in particular. Our Lady was the Mother of the Holy Family, and she gave Jesus to the world. It will never be known on this side of eternity the dignity and the importance of motherhood. Do not all the saints in Heaven owe very much of their sanctity to the holiness of their mothers. If mothers would take Mary for their model, we would find very few souls lost throughout the world. What is badly needed is the supernatural atmosphere in families. We hear also too much of the obligations, the hardships, the difficulties and the responsibilities of mothers, but we do not hear enough of their dignity and the reward that is in store for them. The sanctity of parents is dear to the Immaculate Heart of Mary, and those who are true children of Mary are always preserved from sin and are guarded all through life. If mothers complain of their trials and sorrows, they need only to go back in spirit to the first Christmas night when Mary was repulsed at every door. In haste Mary had to fly into Egypt, and for three days she lost Jesus and sought Him in great sorrow. But the life of Mary was not all sorrow, nor is the life of parents all sorrows or difficulties. The little trials connected with their families are intended to sanctify them and to enable them to obtain abundant graces for the performance of all their duties. Good mothers enjoy great interior peace of soul during life, and in their old age they receive special marks of God's love and protection. In eternity their reward will far surpass even their own expectations, and all the good done by their children will mean additional glory for themselves.

The sweetness of Our Lady is best seen in all times of trouble and difficulty. Some are very much troubled over temporal or worldly matters and yet pay little attention to their sanctification. Very many prayers are unanswered because of the absence of sincerity. We cannot expect the protection of Mary if we continue our sinful lives or if we do not at least strive to overcome our faults. Those who have to fight against temptations have a great helper in Mary—if only they have recourse to her. How many millions of souls have not only been reclaimed from sin but have reached great holiness, simply on account of their having had recourse to the sweet and Immaculate Heart of Mary. It may seem that the purity and goodness of Mary would make her feel disgusted with the baseness of sin, but this is not correct. The saints who preserved all through life their baptismal innocence had the greatest compassion for the poor sinners. Purity increases the love of God and of souls, and Mary wishes above all else the salvation of souls. But once a soul has recourse to this sweet mother, it is so overwhelmed with marks of tenderness that ever afterwards it rests secure under her protection.

When will people learn that it is very easy to secure the friendship of Mary and that her protection destroys all the wiles of the devils. The friendship of Mary is not passing, like so much worldly friendship, which is based often on love of self rather than on love of others. Our Blessed Lady only wishes to bestow graces upon us and to bring us within the Sacred Heart of Jesus. So many wish to be children of the world and children of Mary at the same time. Mary lived in the world for the greater part of her life, and only for a few years was she in the Temple. She does not ask her children to give up the world unless they are called to the religious life. She only wishes them to live interior lives in the midst of all their worldly occupations. This is very easily accomplished by purity of intention and by fervent and frequent prayers. For many years Mary performed only the ordinary duties of domestic life, but these years were all sanctified by her conformity with God's will. It mattered not to her whether she remained in the Temple or cooked a meal, so long as she did God's will. She offered all to God, and she sanctified all her works by prayer. She offered all the little sacrifices of life for the salvation of souls, and in this way all her time was used for increasing her sanctity. Those engaged in any position in life may sanctify themselves by offering all their works to Our Lord in the spirit of penance for the conversion of sinners and by repeating ejaculatory prayers all the day long. These frequent aspirations will sanctify any life and obtain many graces for souls as well as being helpful for the suffering souls in Purgatory.

If parents would only consecrate their children to Mary, they would find that this sweet Mother would not desert them during their lives. Those who are specially consecrated to Mary by becoming a member of her sodality have a sure anchor in all the storms of life. This sweet Mother will never desert them. She may entice some to the cloister and keep others in the world for the bringing up of families and for the sanctification and salvation of souls, but they will never cease to be Mary's children. The Immaculate Heart of Mary will so watch over them that they will become holy almost in spite of themselves. She will use her winning smile of friendship to make them accept her gifts. If they begin to go astray, she will allure them back again with all a mother's affection. She will protect them in all dangers. She will undo all the cunning of the devil, and she will keep them within her mantle for eternity.

> O Mary, my Mother, so tender, so true,
>   In all my afflictions, I hasten to you;
> Your Heart is so gentle, so loving, so mild,
>   You cannot reject your poor suppliant child.

IMMACULATE HEART OF MARY

Gagliardi

THE ASSUMPTION OF THE BLESSED VIRGIN MARY

CHAPTER XXV

The Assumption of the Blessed Virgin

IT IS profitable and interesting to inquire into the reasons for the exultation of the faithful on the occasion of Our Lady's feastdays, and we ought also to know why the Church pays such honors to the Mother of God. To the heretical mind it is bordering on blasphemy to give such manifestations of homage to the Virgin, while to the members of the True Church all this exultation is what is to be expected. The whole difference between the Catholic and the heretic is that the one has the Faith and the other has not. The devil is the author of all heresy, and through want of the means of grace in the case of heretics, it happens that the evil one can so blind their understanding that they are unable to appreciate supernatural truths. To the Catholic these things are easy to understand, simply because his mind is enlightened by God's grace and the devil has not the same power over him. The inveterate enemy of all devotions to the Mother of God is the devil himself, and this is easily explained. The devil held sway over the human race on account of the Fall of our first parents. The promise of a redeemer gave hope of deliverance from the power of the devil. It is easy to see the hatred the devil must have for Mary when we realize that it was through her that all salvation has come to the world.

The most glorious of all her feastdays is the Assumption, which is kept each year on the 15th of August. The Assumption means that the body of Our Lady was not allowed to become corrupt, nor was it allowed to remain in this world long after her death, but that her body was joined again to her soul after death and she was taken body and soul up to Heaven. As Our Lord rose again from the dead on Easter Sunday and went up to Heaven, both Body and Soul, on Ascension Thursday, so is Our Lady's body now in Heaven. The only difference is that Our Lord went up to Heaven visibly, or in the presence of many people on Ascension Thursday; whereas, Our Lady's body was taken up without any public manifestations. It is worthy of note that we have relics in the world of the bodies of the saints. This means that parts of their bodies were picked up and preserved by the faithful after their deaths, but we have no relic of the Body of Our Lord or of His Blessed Mother. These bodies are in Heaven, but the Body of Jesus is also in the Blessed Eucharist.

This Assumption of Our Lady into Heaven fills us with joy and gladness and gives us great reason to have confidence in the midst of all the sorrows in this vale of tears. As Mary ascends to Heaven on that day and as she is raised up in glory above all the saints, many thoughts must pass through her mind. She looks back upon the few years she spent in this world, and what rejoices her more than anything is that she endured so much suffering during these few years. She saw herself filled with the enjoyment of Heaven and of the clear vision of God, and she asked herself how she came to surpass in glory all the saints and patriarchs and martyrs, and she understands for the first time the value of each little suffering borne with and for the sake of her Divine Son. Her Seven Dolors are now seen to be the greatest gifts that her Divine Son could bestow upon her, and she can realize that the desolation and anguish of Good Friday have now brought her this wonderful height of glory. She looks back over the few years in this world and sees now why her Divine Son had sometimes treated her without consideration, especially in the case of the three days' loss and during the years without any consolation or encouragement. She sees now why on this earth she received no honors nor applause. All these crosses were given to her to carry in order to increase the state of Sanctifying Grace in her soul and so that she might enjoy for eternity the unalloyed glories of the New Jerusalem.

Perhaps there is no feast of the year from which we can derive so much consolation as from this feast of Our Lady's Assumption. As Mary grew in years, she was also growing in grace, and her Assumption is the crowning of her life work and her sufferings. She was raised then to the highest place in Heaven simply because her soul was prepared by grace for such an eminence of glory. This grace and all these dignities were well earned during her life on earth. No child of Adam bore such sufferings as Mary, after those of her Divine Son, and no child of Adam reaches her in the glory of Paradise, for she is next to her Divine Son. Oh, what a subject for deep reflection and for daily meditation! The glory of Heaven will correspond exactly with our sufferings and humiliations and with the patience with which we bear all the trials of this short life. Jesus could very well have kept Mary away from Calvary on the first Good Friday. She had never appeared in His triumph during the years of His Public Life. But Jesus wanted Mary to share in His sufferings so that He would have her near Him for the eternal years. What a pity that so many murmur so in their crosses and disappointments of this life, when in reality Our Lord only wishes to sanctify them for the eternal possession of Himself in Heaven.

Another reason for the glories of Mary is to make her power of intercession very great for the salvation of souls. Our Lord still intercedes for us daily by renewing the Sacrifice of Calvary through the Sacrifice of the Mass. But so many will not make use of Our Lord's sufferings, nor will they take advantage of Our Lord's Presence in the Blessed Eucharist. It is a great act of charity to pray for these poor souls, and it means the salvation of many souls to have someone who is powerful enough to intercede for them. The "Communion of Saints" means that the faithful on earth, the suffering in Purgatory, and the triumphant in Heaven can assist each other and that we can appeal to the saints to pray for us. Prayer is a sure way to obtain God's grace, but the prayers of those who are near to God, whether in this world or in Heaven, are much more powerful than those who are less perfect or who are devoid of grace. The more grace possessed by a soul the more powerful are her prayers, and this holds with the faithful on earth and with the saints in Heaven. Our Lady has been raised up so high in glory that a single prayer from her disarms all the powers of Hell and foils all the plans of the devil. The devil hates devotion to Mary, and for a very good reason. Those who are children of Mary and those who frequently invoke her, or honor her by keeping specially her feasts, are sure of being aided by her prayers. As surely as Mary prays for a soul, that soul is safe! As surely as we become children of Mary, not only is our salvation secure, but we are assured of her special protection all through life and at the hour of death. In this way we are safe from all the powers of Hell, because a single prayer from Mary puts the devils to flight and spoils all their hateful devices.

From the feast of the Assumption we can learn very many profitable lessons. In the first place, we can realize the value of sufferings patiently borne for the love of Jesus. We ought to offer all our sufferings in the spirit of penance in union with the sufferings of Jesus on the Cross, and if we offer them like Jesus and Mary for the salvation of souls, we will thereby cooperate with Jesus in the work of Redemption. In the second place, we ought to have a tender devotion to Mary and become her children by performing those works of devotion which will secure for us her protection and the grace of God. These are principally praying her Rosary, wearing her Scapulars, keeping her feasts, joining those sodalities erected in her honor, and having great zeal for souls. We can at least pray much for the conversion of sinners and for the spread of the Faith. Her Son died to save souls, and we can please Mary by offering our prayers and sufferings for the salvation of souls. It is good also to look often up to Heaven and not think too much upon the passing things of this world.

O joyful heart of Mary,
  What trembling bliss was thine,
Thy Son and God to worship
  Within His humble shrine:
To watch His Infant footsteps,
  To guard His Infant rest,
Within thine arms to shield Him
  And clasp Him to thy breast.

O mournful Heart of Mary,
  To meet that cruel day,
When rent and racked and tortured,
  Upon the Cross He lay;
To feel His bitter anguish,
  To hear His dying cry,
To see His death thirst mocked at
  And then to see Him die.

O glorious Heart of Mary,
  O wonder spot above,
Where God hath all surpassed Himself
  In royalty and love;
For every pang a glory,
  For every prayer a wreath,
His crowning grace above thee,
  His brightest saints beneath.

But sweetest and joyful Mother,
  Mother of tears and woe,
Mother of grace and glory,
  Thou still hast cares below:
Then bid us share thy rapture,
  And bid us taste the pain,
And sing at last thy grandeur
  In Christ's eternal reign.

THE END

THE SORROWFUL MOTHER

APPENDIX

The Little Rosary
Of the Seven Dolors of Mary

With Meditations by St. Alphonsus Liguori (optional)

V. Incline unto mine aid, O God.
R. O Lord, make haste to help me.

Glory be to the Father, and to the Son, and to the Holy Ghost: as it was in the beginning, is now, and ever shall be, world without end. *Amen.*

Strophe: My Mother, share thy grief with me,
And let me bear thee company
To mourn thy Jesus' death with thee.

Meditation on the First Dolor: I pity thee, O afflicted Mother, on account of the first sword of sorrow which pierced thee, when in the Temple all the outrages which men would inflict on thy beloved Jesus were presented before thee by Saint Simeon, and which thou didst already know by the Sacred Scriptures; outrages which were to cause Him to die before thine eyes, on an infamous Cross, exhausted of His blood, abandoned by all, and thyself unable to defend or help Him. By that bitter knowledge, then, which for so many years afflicted thy heart, I beseech thee, my Queen, to obtain for me the grace that during my life and at my death I may ever keep the Passion of Jesus and thy sorrows impressed upon my heart.

Our Father, seven Hail Marys, and the Strophe are repeated after each Dolor.

Meditation on the Second Dolor: I pity thee, my afflicted Mother, for the second sword which pierced thee, when soon after His birth thou didst behold thine innocent Son threatened with death by those very men for whose salvation He had come into the world, so that in the darkness of night thou wast obliged to fly secretly with Him into Egypt. By the many hardships, then, which thou, a delicate young woman, in company with thine exiled Child, didst endure in so long and fatiguing a journey through rough and desert countries, and during thy residence in Egypt, where, being unknown and a stranger, thou didst live for so many years in poverty and contempt—I beseech thee, my beloved Lady, to obtain for me the grace to suffer in thy company with patience until death the trials of this miserable life, that I may thus in the next escape the eternal punishments of Hell, which I have deserved.

Our Father, seven Hail Marys and the Strophe.

Meditation on the Third Dolor: I pity thee, my sorrowful Mother, on account of the third sword which pierced thee in the loss of thy dear Son Jesus, who remained absent from thee in Jerusalem for three days. No longer seeing thy Beloved by thy side and not knowing the cause of His absence, I can well imagine, my loving Queen, that during those nights thou didst not repose and didst only sigh for Him, who was all thy treasure. By the sighs, then, of those three days, for thee too long and bitter, I beseech thee to obtain for me the grace that I may never lose my God, that so, always clinging to Him, I may leave the world united to Him.

Our Father, seven Hail Marys and the Strophe.

Meditation on the Fourth Dolor: I pity thee, my sorrowful Mother, for the fourth sword which pierced thee in seeing thy Son condemned to death, bound with cords and chains, covered with blood and wounds, crowned with a wreath of thorns, falling under the heavy weight of the Cross which He carried on His wounded shoulders, going as an innocent Lamb to die for love of us. Thine eyes met His, and His met thine; and thy glances were as so many cruel arrows which wounded thy loving hearts. By this great sorrow, then, I beseech thee to obtain for me the grace to live in all things resigned to the will of my God and to carry my cross cheerfully in company with Jesus, until my last breath.

Our Father, seven Hail Marys and the Strophe.

Meditation on the Fifth Dolor: I pity thee, my afflicted Mother, for the fifth sword which pierced thee, when on Mount Calvary thou didst behold thy beloved Son Jesus slowly dying before thine eyes, amid so many torments and insults, on that hard bed of the Cross, where thou couldst not administer to Him even the least of those comforts which are granted to the greatest criminals at the hour of death. I beseech thee by the agony which thou, my most loving Mother, didst endure, together with thy dying Son, and by the sadness which thou didst feel when, for the last time, He spoke to thee from the Cross and bade thee farewell and left all of us in the person of Saint John to thee as thy children; by that constancy with which thou didst then see Him bow down His head and expire, I beseech thee to obtain for me the grace from thy crucified Love to live and die crucified to all earthly things, that I may spend my life for God alone and thus one day enter Paradise to enjoy Him face to face.

Our Father, seven Hail Marys and the Strophe.

Meditation on the Sixth Dolor: I pity thee, my afflicted Mother, for the sixth sword which pierced thee when thou didst see the sweet heart of thy Son pierced through and through. He was already dead and had died for those ungrateful creatures who, even after His death, were not satisfied with the torments they had inflicted upon Him. By this cruel sorrow, then, which was all thine, I beseech thee to obtain for me the grace to dwell in the heart of Jesus, wounded and opened for me; in that heart, I say, which is the beautiful abode of love, in which all souls who love God repose; and that, living there, I may never think of or love anything but God. Most sacred Virgin, thou canst obtain this for me; from thee do I hope for it.

Our Father, seven Hail Marys and the Strophe.

Meditation on the Seventh Dolor: I pity thee, my afflicted Mother, for the seventh sword which pierced thee on seeing thy Son already dead in thy arms, no longer fair and beautiful as thou didst receive Him in the stable of Bethlehem, but covered with blood, livid and all lacerated with wounds, so that even His bones were seen; thou didst then say, "My Son, my Son, to what has love reduced Thee!" And when He was borne to the sepulcher, thou wouldst thyself accompany Him and place Him with thine own hands in the tomb; and bidding Him thy last farewell, thou didst leave thy loving heart buried with thy Son. By this martyrdom of thy beautiful soul, do thou obtain for me, O Mother of Fair Love, the forgiveness of the offences which I have committed against my beloved God, and which I repent with my whole heart. Do thou defend me in temptations; do thou assist me at the moment of my death, that, saving my soul through the merits of Jesus and thee, I may one day, after this miserable exile, go to Paradise to sing the praises of Jesus and of thee for all eternity. *Amen.*

Our Father, seven Hail Marys and the Strophe.

V. Pray for us, O most sorrowful Virgin,

R. That we may be made worthy of the promises of Christ.

Let us pray.

O God, at whose Passion, according to the prophecy of Simeon, a sword of sorrow didst pierce through the most sweet soul of the glorious Virgin and Mother Mary, grant that we who commemorate and reverence her dolors may experience the blessed effect of Thy Passion, who livest and reignest world without end. *Amen.*

THE MOTHER OF SORROWS

OUR LADY OF GRACE

If you have enjoyed this book, consider making your next selection from among the following . . .

Prices subject to change.

Moments Divine—Before the Blessed Sacrament. *Reuter* 8.50
Miraculous Images of Our Lady. *Cruz* 20.00
Miraculous Images of Our Lord. *Cruz* 13.50
Raised from the Dead. *Fr. Hebert*. 16.50
Love and Service of God, Infinite Love. *Mother Louise Margaret* 12.50
Life and Work of Mother Louise Margaret. *Fr. O'Connell* 12.50
Autobiography of St. Margaret Mary. 5.00
Thoughts and Sayings of St. Margaret Mary 5.00
The Voice of the Saints. *Comp. by Francis Johnston* 6.00
The 12 Steps to Holiness and Salvation. *St. Alphonsus*. 7.50
The Rosary and the Crisis of Faith. *Cirrincione & Nelson* 2.00
Sin and Its Consequences. *Cardinal Manning* 6.00
Fourfold Sovereignty of God. *Cardinal Manning* 5.00
Dialogue of St. Catherine of Siena. *Transl. Algar Thorold* 10.00
Catholic Answer to Jehovah's Witnesses. *D'Angelo* 10.00
Twelve Promises of the Sacred Heart. (100 cards). 5.00
Life of St. Aloysius Gonzaga. *Fr. Meschler* 12.00
The Love of Mary. *D. Roberto*. 8.00
Begone Satan. *Fr. Vogl*. 3.00
The Prophets and Our Times. *Fr. R. G. Culleton* 12.50
St. Therese, The Little Flower. *John Beevers* 6.00
St. Joseph of Copertino. *Fr. Angelo Pastrovicchi* 6.00
Mary, The Second Eve. *Cardinal Newman*. 2.50
Devotion to Infant Jesus of Prague. *Booklet*. 75
Reign of Christ the King in Public & Private Life. *Davies* 1.25
The Wonder of Guadalupe. *Francis Johnston*. 7.50
Apologetics. *Msgr. Paul Glenn*. 10.00
Baltimore Catechism No. 1. . . . . 3.50
Baltimore Catechism No. 2. . . . . 4.50
Baltimore Catechism No. 3. . . . . 8.00
An Explanation of the Baltimore Catechism. *Fr. Kinkead*. 16.50
Bethlehem. *Fr. Faber*. 18.00
Bible History. *Schuster*. 10.00
Blessed Eucharist. *Fr. Mueller*. 9.00
Catholic Catechism. *Fr. Faerber* 7.00
The Devil. *Fr. Delaporte* 6.00
Dogmatic Theology for the Laity. *Fr. Premm* 20.00
Evidence of Satan in the Modern World. *Cristiani* 10.00
Fifteen Promises of Mary. (100 cards). 5.00
Life of Anne Catherine Emmerich. 2 vols. *Schmoeger* 37.50
Life of the Blessed Virgin Mary. *Emmerich* 16.50
Manual of Practical Devotion to St. Joseph. *Patrignani* 15.00
Prayer to St. Michael. (100 leaflets) 5.00
Prayerbook of Favorite Litanies. *Fr. Hebert* 10.00
Preparation for Death. (Abridged). *St. Alphonsus* 8.00
Purgatory Explained. *Schouppe* 13.50
Purgatory Explained. (pocket, unabr.). *Schouppe* 9.00
Fundamentals of Catholic Dogma. *Ludwig Ott*. 21.00
Spiritual Conferences. *Tauler*. 13.00
Trustful Surrender to Divine Providence. *Bl. Claude* 5.00
Wife, Mother and Mystic. *Bessieres*. 8.00
The Agony of Jesus. *Padre Pio* 1.50

Prices subject to change.

Prices subject to change.

Hail Holy Queen (from *Glories of Mary*). *St. Alphonsus* 8.00
Novena of Holy Communions. *Lovasik* 2.00
Brief Catechism for Adults. *Cogan*. 9.00
The Cath. Religion—Illus./Expl. for Child, Adult, Convert. *Burbach* 9.00
Eucharistic Miracles. *Joan Carroll Cruz* 15.00
The Incorruptibles. *Joan Carroll Cruz* 13.50
Pope St. Pius X. *F. A. Forbes* 8.00
St. Alphonsus Liguori. *Frs. Miller and Aubin*. 16.50
Self-Abandonment to Divine Providence. *Fr. de Caussade, S.J.* 18.00
The Song of Songs—A Mystical Exposition. *Fr. Arintero, O.P.* 20.00
Prophecy for Today. *Edward Connor* 5.50
Saint Michael and the Angels. *Approved Sources* 7.00
Dolorous Passion of Our Lord. *Anne C. Emmerich*. 16.50
Modern Saints—Their Lives & Faces, Book I. *Ann Ball* 18.00
Modern Saints—Their Lives & Faces, Book II. *Ann Ball*. 20.00
Our Lady of Fatima's Peace Plan from Heaven. *Booklet* .... .75
Divine Favors Granted to St. Joseph. *Père Binet* 5.00
St. Joseph Cafasso—Priest of the Gallows. *St. John Bosco*. 4.50
Catechism of the Council of Trent. *McHugh/Callan*. 24.00
The Foot of the Cross. *Fr. Faber*. 16.50
The Rosary in Action. *John Johnson* 9.00
Padre Pio—The Stigmatist. *Fr. Charles Carty* 15.00
Why Squander Illness? *Frs. Rumble & Carty*. 2.00
The Sacred Heart and the Priesthood. *de la Touche* 9.00
Fatima—The Great Sign. *Francis Johnston* 8.00
Heliotropium—Conformity of Human Will to Divine. *Drexelius* 13.00
Charity for the Suffering Souls. *Fr. John Nageleisen* 16.50
Devotion to the Sacred Heart of Jesus. *Verheylezoon* 15.00
Who Is Padre Pio? *Radio Replies Press* 1.50
Child's Bible History. *Knecht*. 4.00
The Stigmata and Modern Science. *Fr. Charles Carty* 1.25
The Life of Christ. 4 Vols. H.B. *Anne C. Emmerich* 60.00
St. Anthony—The Wonder Worker of Padua. *Stoddard* 5.00
The Precious Blood. *Fr. Faber*. 13.50
The Holy Shroud & Four Visions. *Fr. O'Connell* 2.00
Clean Love in Courtship. *Fr. Lawrence Lovasik*. 2.50
The Prophecies of St. Malachy. *Peter Bander*. 7.00
St. Martin de Porres. *Giuliana Cavallini* 12.50
The Secret of the Rosary. *St. Louis De Montfort*. 3.00
The History of Antichrist. *Rev. P. Huchede*. 4.00
St. Catherine of Siena. *Alice Curtayne* 13.50
Where We Got the Bible. *Fr. Henry Graham* 6.00
Hidden Treasure—Holy Mass. *St. Leonard*. 5.00
Imitation of the Sacred Heart of Jesus. *Fr. Arnoudt* 15.00
The Life & Glories of St. Joseph. *Edward Thompson*. 15.00
Père Lamy. *Biver*. 10.00
Humility of Heart. *Fr. Cajetan da Bergamo* 8.50
The Curé D'Ars. *Abbé Francis Trochu*. 21.50
Love, Peace and Joy. (St. Gertrude). *Prévot* 7.00

At your Bookdealer or direct from the Publisher.
Call Toll-Free 1-800-437-5876.

Prices subject to change.

GIVE COPIES OF THIS BOOK...

To friends and relatives, to priests and bishops, to nuns and religious, to members of your parish and religious group, to high school and college students, to the religiously committed and the fallen away, to Catholics and non-Catholics, to teachers and educators, to molders of public opinion and political leaders, to Protestants and Jews, to atheists and agnostics—in short, you can give this book to anyone. Everyone has heard about the Blessed Virgin Mary. But very few really understand her exalted role in our redemption and in our salvation. Very few today realize or recognize her tremendous spiritual power. According to the revelations of many saints, it will only be through the intercession of Mary that our modern world will ever achieve peace and reconciliation with God. It is only through Mary that many people will be saved at all. Absence of knowledge about Mary works to the harm of us all in that our world is poorer, more sinful, and increasingly chaotic as a result. Knowledge of Mary brings consolation to hearts and love to souls. Knowledge of Mary inspires people to virtue and to hope in God. Knowledge of Mary truly insures supernatural faith and true Christian charity. Knowledge of Mary, in short, transforms the heart and the mind and brings people humbly to the feet of Jesus to seek forgiveness and the grace to lead a new life. Knowledge of Mary is what our poor, sick, weary world needs most, for knowledge of Mary will lead to true faith. Consequently, it behooves every reader inspired by this book to obtain extra copies to pass out to others. The issue is the salvation of souls and peace in the world. Order your copies today and help spread the knowledge of Mary. Help spread the True Faith. Help bring others to reconciliation with God and true peace to our tired and sinful world.

Quantity Discount

1 copy	$10.00	
5 copies	6.00 each	30.00 total
10 copies	5.00 each	50.00 total

Priced low for widespread distribution.

ORDER FORM

(Tear out and mail)

TAN BOOKS AND PUBLISHERS, INC.
P.O. Box 424
Rockford, Illinois 61105

Gentlemen:

Please send me _____ copies of **The Mother of God and Her**

Glorious Feasts by Fr. H. O'Laverty, B.A.

Enclosed is my payment in the amount of _____ .

Name _____

Street _____

City _____

State _____ Zip _____

Alternate Payment Plan

Please charge to my _____ VISA _____ Mastercard.

My Account No. is _____

My card expires (give month and year) _____

Signature _____

(Do not send us your card.)

Please include postage and handling according to the following: For orders of $1-$20, add $3; $20.01-$30, add $4; $30.01-$50, add $5; $50.01-$75, add $6; $75.01-up, add $7. Illinois residents add 6% Sales Tax. All foreign customers please remit in U.S. funds. Overseas customers add 20% of your order for surface postage. Tel. Toll Free: 1-800-437-5876.